The Abingdon Preaching Annual
2023

The Abingdon
Preaching Annual

2023

Planning Sermons
for Fifty-Two Sundays

Charley Reeb, General Editor

Abingdon Press™

Nashville

THE ABINGDON PREACHING ANNUAL 2023:
PLANNING SERMONS FOR FIFTY-TWO SUNDAYS

Copyright © 2022 by Abingdon Press

ISBN 978-1-7910-2380-5

Scripture quotations unless noted otherwise are from the Common English Bible. Copyright © 2011 by the Common English Bible. All rights reserved. Used by permission. www.CommonEnglishBible.com.

Scripture quotations marked (NIV) are taken from the Holy Bible, New International Version®, NIV®. Copyright © 1973, 1978, 1984, 2011 by Biblica, Inc.™ Used by permission of Zondervan. All rights reserved worldwide. www.zondervan.com The "NIV" and "New International Version" are trademarks registered in the United States Patent and Trademark Office by Biblica, Inc.™

Scripture quotations marked (NRSV) are taken from the New Revised Standard Version of the Bible, copyright 1989, Division of Christian Education of the National Council of the Churches of Christ in the United States of America. Used by permission. All rights reserved.

The excerpt on pages 153–55 is taken from Will Willimon's *Listeners Dare: Hearing God in the Sermon*, published by Abingdon Press in 2022.

The excerpt on pages 156–60 is taken from Karoline M. Lewis's *Embody: Five Keys to Leading with Integrity*, published by Abingdon Press in 2020.

The excerpt on pages 161–70 is taken from Frank A. Thomas's *The God of the Dangerous Sermon*, published by Abingdon Press in 2021.

22 23 24 25 26 27 28 29 30 31 — 10 9 8 7 6 5 4 3 2 1
MANUFACTURED IN THE UNITED STATES OF AMERICA

Contents

🌿 = Sunday in Lent   ☠ = Sunday of Advent

ESSAYS FOR SKILL-BUILDING

Preface

It is my joy to offer you the 2023 edition of the *Abingdon Preaching Annual*. As always, you will find insightful and inspirational material that will provide invaluable help in the preparation of sermons. You may have noticed that the 2022 edition had a change in format. The same approach is also found in this edition. Instead of incorporating all of the selected readings, each entry focuses primarily on a single text. We find this is more helpful for preachers who typically choose one text for their sermon and desire a deeper reflection on the chosen passage. "Worship Helps" are also absent to provide more room for practical guidance and illustrations for sermons ("Bringing the Text to Life"). We believe a more vigorous treatment of a single text is beneficial for busy preachers who need their time preparing sermons to be both fruitful and efficient. If you are looking for worship material, the *Abingdon Worship Annual* is an excellent resource.

This helpful book would never see the light of day if it wasn't for the very capable team of editors at Abingdon Press. Many thanks to them for bringing this resource to life.

Charley Reeb
General Editor

Sermon Helps

January 1, 2023–New Year's Day

Ecclesiastes 3:1-13; Psalm 8; Revelation 21:1-6a; **Matthew 25:31-46**

Jennifer Forrester

Preacher to Preacher Prayer

Gracious God, may all that we do be done in love, expecting nothing in return for ourselves. And may all that we do for those in whom we consider the least of these be done without placing ourselves at odds with those we consider to be rich, and with whom we don't agree. Rather, let us serve for your sake alone. Amen.

Commentary

"When you have done it for one of the least of these brothers and sisters of mine, you have done it for me" (v. 40). These are familiar words for most of us. Most preachers have preached or taught this verse at some point in their ministry. I guess you can say we are drawn to it. Maybe we like the simplicity of it or the way it makes us feel good about the things we are doing for others, if we are indeed doing them. We can pat ourselves on the back and call ourselves "good sheep." But are we? Is it really that simple, or do we oversimplify it because we fail to have the imagination for the rich imagery Jesus is using here to make his point?

This is the final parable Jesus will tell in the Gospel of Matthew before he faces his own judgment. Jesus is giving us one last point of clarification in case we still haven't understood. It is as if Jesus says, "This is it! All the words I have said can be summed up in this: if you forget everything else I've taught you, here it is one last time." When it is all said and done, "when the Human One comes in his majesty and all his angels are with him, he will sit on his majestic throne" (v. 31), and each will stand before him and be judged. Now, I'm not sure about you, but I don't necessarily like the way that sounds, but it's simple, right?

The imagery Jesus uses is the nations being gathered and separated into two groups. Jesus has returned and stands before them as the Great Shepherd, the image Matthew uses throughout his Gospel when depicting Jesus. The flocks throughout Palestine during this time were often mixed herds, consisting of both sheep and goats.

At night the sheep and goats often had to be separated because goats couldn't be left in the cold. The sheep, however, would rather be in the open air. Sheep were also preferred because they were of more value than that of their goat pasture-mates.

So, the nations are standing before the Son of Man. In other words, each of us is standing before Jesus, fully seen, with all of our agendas, mixed motives, and broken relationships, and we're asked one simple question. But is it really that simple? When I read Fred Craddock's sermon on this scripture titled "When He Shall Come," I began to think differently. Craddock said, "When I listen to people talk, sincere and dedicated members of various churches, it is seldom that I hear a discussion that centers upon this question, which is, in the mind of God, the ultimate question."[1] We all hope we'll be judged in another way. In our society today, we talk more about the sins of the world. We have a long list of those. We even like to give some sins more weight than others, hoping to separate ourselves from the "goats." But, sin is not what is included in this final judgment. Jesus asks one question. When did you?

When did you ask me how you could help when I felt all alone in this world; as a single mom doing all I could to keep a roof over my kids' heads, crying myself to sleep every night because I was tired, lonely, and afraid?

When did you introduce yourself to me when I walked into your church wearing that old brown coat and tattered ball cap and made everyone feel uneasy because of the lost look in my eyes? I just wanted to know that someone could care about me too.

When did you continue to offer me and the others like me (very different from you) a meal even when the neighbor down the street scowled, accused, and made complaints about me?

That's the question. When? That's the judgment according to this familiar scripture that we all are drawn to in Matthew's Gospel. Simple enough.

Bringing the Text to Life

Years ago, when I first answered my call to ministry, I began as a youth director. I quickly sought out mission opportunities to get the youth involved in serving others. I have always felt that it is through relationships and serving others that we can not only share Christ but can experience Christ like never before. I came across a mission camp, "M25," led by a man named Gabe Barrett. My youth group attended this camp for years while I was their leader.

On our first night there that first year, Gabe told a story of his time out in Los Angeles after he graduated from college. He said he was trying to discover himself and what he was to do in this life. He decided to volunteer down at skid row in the soup kitchen, serving folks food and even cleaning toilets. One evening he left the soup kitchen feeling extremely overwhelmed so his buddy took him on a hike. The trail ended on the edge of a mountain looking over all of LA. Gabe could see the vast city for miles, even the iconic "Hollywood" sign in the distance. He stood looking over the millions of lights below him and felt helpless. He said, "God, what can I possibly do? I can't change this world." He stood for a moment and what he heard back was "Gabe, you don't have to change the world, just change someone's day."

Maybe that is the final question for us. When did you change someone's day?

January 8, 2023–Baptism of the Lord–First Sunday after the Epiphany

*Isaiah 42:1-9; Psalm 29; **Acts 10:34-43**; Matthew 3:13-17*

Jennifer Forrester

Preacher to Preacher Prayer

Gracious and loving God, thank you for the gift of the Holy Spirit that descends upon each of us just as it did on the day of Jesus's baptism. God, by the power of Your spirit, remind us of your call and continue to guide us, we pray. Amen.

Commentary

Often, I feel, when we read the prescribed lectionary text, we are left feeling as if something is missing, like perhaps we are missing part of the story. Some key words that start the weekly text that might cause this feeling are words like *then, after,* or in this week's pericope, *Peter said . . .* In order to understand why Peter is saying, we need to know where the story began.

If we go back to the beginning of chapter 10 in the book of Acts, we meet Cornelius, a pious Caesarean centurion. We are told that he and his whole household are "Gentile God-worshippers" (v. 2). Cornelius is visited by an angel who recognizes his compassion for others and tells him to go call for Peter. Cornelius, being a devout, religious man, does what he is told by the angel and sends two of his servants for Peter. As they are nearing Joppa the next day, Peter goes up to the rooftop to pray, and while there becomes hungry. It might not seem like the best place for a picnic, but Peter's vision is one from God, lowering what appears to be a large sheet full of all kinds of nonkosher creatures that God tells him to kill and eat.

Peter, being a devout follower of Jewish law, denies the offer in his typical three-time fashion. What Peter doesn't realize though is that he almost misses a message from God that changes the course for the followers of Jesus. By showing more concern for ritual, as they pertain to religious dietary regulations, he almost misses the message from God that God doesn't show one group of people partiality over another. What Peter almost missed was that his vision was about much more than food. When he finally gets it, well, that's where we pick up in this week's text. Peter says, "Every nation, whoever worships him and does what is right is acceptable to him" (v. 35). And then he reminds them, "This is the message of peace he sent to the Israelites by proclaiming the good news through Jesus Christ: He is Lord of all!" (v. 36).

Peter, with his mind and heart changed, says God shows no partiality (v. 34). Willie Jennings, in his commentary on Acts, says it this way: "God's tastes are much wider than Peter had imagined until this moment. Peter is at the threshold of revelation. The revelation is not of God's wider palette for people, but that Peter's range of whom to love and desire must expand until it stretches beyond his own limits into God's life."[2]

On this Baptism of the Lord Sunday I wonder if we can feel Peter's conviction? Peter says, "We are witnesses of everything he did" (v. 39), his life, his death, and his resurrection. Peter says, "We are witnesses whom God chose beforehand, who ate and drank with him after God raised him from the dead" (v. 41). Peter is reminding them that Jesus commanded them to preach to all people that everyone who believes in him will receive forgiveness.

Peter reminded the people gathered there, Jew and Gentile, of Jesus's baptism and how he was empowered by the Holy Spirit to go and do and proclaim. May every song we sing, every testimony we share, and every act of love we offer be in the name of Christ. And may we also be reminded that through our baptism we are people who are joined to other people by the power of the Holy Spirit. May we feel Peter's same conviction.

Bringing the Text to Life

When our children were little, my husband and I spent a lot of time camping. We had the whole set-up: the camper, the camp chairs, the bicycles and all the riding toys. And when we would camp at the beach we'd throw in the kiddie pool and beach toys, too. One year while camping in Panama City Beach, when our oldest child was about three and a half years old, we were all hanging out at the camper taking a break from the afternoon sun waiting for his baby sister to wake up from her nap. She had just woken up and was sitting in my lap in one of the camp chairs. Our son was splashing around in the kiddie pool when all of a sudden he crouched down in the kiddie pool, filled his little hands with water, and as he raised up he threw the water in the air toward us and said, "Remember your baptism and be thankful." He had gotten that from one of our pastors at the time. Every time there was a baptism in the church, the pastor would gather water in his hands from the baptismal font, throw it out onto the congregation and say, "Remember your baptism and be thankful."

Our scripture today reminds us of our call as baptized believers of Jesus Christ to go. By the power of the Holy Spirit, we are to go, just as Peter and the disciples were to go and proclaim the good news of Jesus Christ to all.

January 15, 2023–Second Sunday after the Epiphany

Isaiah 49:1-7; *Psalm 40:1-11; 1 Corinthians 1:1-9; John 1:29-42*

Jennifer Forrester

Preacher to Preacher Prayer

Gracious God, just as you spoke to the prophets reminding them that there was still work to be done, remind us today. Remind us that you will provide all that we need for the tasks you are calling us to. Guide us and grant us your peace and assurance. Amen.

Commentary

The entire story of the Bible is God seeking to be back in right relationship with all of creation. This text from Isaiah is the reminder of the call to the suffering servant, "The Holy One of Israel, who has chosen you" (v. 7). So, the question is, who then is the servant? Well, at first glance it appears to be Israel. Verse 3 says, "You are my servant, Israel, in whom I show my glory." But a little later it seems that the servant is supposed to save Israel. So, which is it? It seems a little odd to me that part of Israel's mission is to save Israel. Theologian Walter Brueggemann says, "It may be that the poem deliberately avoids naming a specific identity, thus giving us great freedom in our hearing."[3] "In this text coming from second Isaiah," according to the writer of "The Interpretation" commentary on Isaiah, "the nation or people Israel are often designated as servant."[4] Therefore, the servant could be Isaiah, Jeremiah, or Elijah. The servant could be referring to the people who continue to remain faithful in Israel, or it could be the entire community who still lives there. To narrow it down to one person is difficult. I believe to make it relevant to our congregations and people today, the servant has to be us.

If we read this scripture naming "us" as the servant, what do we hear? Well, I hear both comfort and call. In the midst of exile, the word of God has come to give people hope, but there is the reminder that God's people do not exist only for themselves, nor is their restoration an end in itself. God says that this restoration of Israel "is not enough" (v. 6). God's focus isn't for our own resolutions to our own personal crises and then God's work is done, like we often believe. I do believe God cares about our individual well-being, but that's not where the story ends. That's only the beginning. God's healing work moves inward but doesn't stop there. God's restoration is always expanding outward, "so that my salvation may reach to the end of the earth" (v. 6). God's story is always bigger than ours, holding our stories within God's life and weaving them into the wide-open future.

But, this is hard work and it's not a small task. Being called, I don't think, ever is. The servant is being called to a people in crisis, a people unsure of their own identity, and even their faith. It sounds a lot like our world today. There's a looming question that I see and that is, how can people living in a time like they were worship? How can we, living today, worship? It is easy to get overwhelmed with all that the world throws at us. It's easy to believe we have nothing to do or say to make any kind of difference. The unidentified servant had been doing the work for a while, it seems, continually encountering frustration and disappointment: "I have wearied myself in vain. I have used up my strength for nothing" (Isa 49:4). And, haven't we all felt this? We, as the church, are doing ministry to the best of our ability, yet we don't seem to be getting anywhere. We focus on love, grace, and forgiveness, and there are still those who don't feel as if they are welcome. There seems to be more separation than ever before despite our message of oneness in Christ.

The struggle continues to be real, yet God says, "God . . . hid me in the shadow of God's own hand" (v. 2). To be held in the shadows of God's hands . . . what a beautiful image that is. God's suffering servant being protected somehow. It's hard work recognizing ourselves as servants of God. If it's hard enough for those of us who feel called to ministry as a vocation, we can then imagine it to be even harder for members of our congregation, our churches, and our communities.

This scripture from Isaiah should give us a renewed sense of call reminding us that God is not yet done. God is not yet done with us or the world that God created and loves.

Bringing the Text to Life

There are people in this world whom I have never met, yet who have had a great impact on my life and call. I'm guessing you can think of a few people like that in your life, too.

There is a pastor in the Western North Carolina Conference who is no longer living, yet he lives on. Through his family, who are almost all Methodist pastors as well, and people in whom he had an impact through his life of ministry and service to others, I have heard stories that have made me want to love people better and I have been uplifted by scriptures that he too leaned on in "suffering servant" times.

The call from this scripture is not only for our own restoration. Verse 6 says, "I will also appoint you as light to the nations so that my salvation may reach to the end of the earth." I believe we are called to be the light, each and every one, a light that continues to shine beyond right now.

Maybe the question for us, and our congregations, should be, what are we doing now that shines light on something beyond ourselves?

January 22, 2023—Third Sunday after the Epiphany

Isaiah 9:1-4; Psalm 27:1, 4-9; 1 Corinthians 1:10-18; **Matthew 4:12-23**

Bill Burch

Preacher to Preacher Prayer

God of light and love, illumine my human words with your divine Word. Fill this earthen jar with heavenly treasures. Grant eyes to see your coming kingdom, ears to hear your guiding voice, lips to share your good news, and feet to follow your guidance. Amen.

Commentary

Following Jesus's temptation in the wilderness, the Lord learns of John the Baptist's arrest. (Unlike Luke, Matthew does not mention the poignant fact that the two are cousins.) Jesus leaves his hometown of Nazareth and withdraws to Galilee, settling in Capernaum. (A geographic mnemonic teaches "Capernaum CAPS the Sea of Galilee!")

Matthew writes for a Jewish audience and never misses a chance to prooftext a messianic prophecy. (Hey, who hasn't?) The author quotes Isaiah 9:1-4, taking some liberties with the script. In the original text, the light appearing in the darkness might have symbolized a royal birth or enthronement. Matthew repurposes the passage to support the Messiah's dawning ministry in Galilee.

Matthew 4:17 gives a summary of Jesus's inaugural message, "Change your hearts and lives! Here comes the kingdom of heaven!"

The CEB version replaces the rich, theological term "repent" with "change your hearts and lives." What is gained and lost in the translation? "Here comes the kingdom of heaven" lacks the nuance of alternate translations like "the kingdom of heaven is at hand" or "the kingdom of heaven has come near."

Ultimately, the proximity of heaven's kingdom cannot be ascertained in geographic or temporal terms. It possesses a "here" but "not yet" quality. English does not allow grammarians to conjugate nouns, but heaven's kingdom encompasses past, present, and future tenses. It has come, is coming, and will come.

As a devotional, theological, and homiletical exercise, compare and contrast the four Gospels. Mark and Luke record Jesus preaching about "the kingdom of God." However, Matthew substitutes "heaven" for "God" to appease Jewish sensibilities. In a radical departure from the Synoptic Gospels, John emphasizes "eternal life" instead.

Matthew juxtaposes Isaiah's prophecy and Jesus's sermon. How do the passages inform one another? In the gospel context, Jesus appears as a great light in the darkness and in the shadow of death. The imagery also gives insight into the dawning nature of heaven's kingdom.

Matthew 4:18-22 summarizes the call of the first disciples. Jesus encounters two brothers, Simon (nicknamed Peter; Matt 16:13-20 [SPOILER ALERT!]) and Andrew. Matthew does not record any previous encounters. However, John's Gospel portrays Andrew as a disciple of John the Baptist. Andrew introduces Simon to Jesus. Regardless, one assumes some prior interaction between Jesus and the two brothers.

Hear the refreshing simplicity of Jesus's initial call, "Come, follow me." Then he adds the enticing invitation, "I'll show you how to fish for people" (v. 19). From the start, Christ inseparably interlinks discipleship and evangelism.

The job description changes later with "other duties as assigned." On the road to Jerusalem's cross, Christ challenges his disciples to deny self, take up the cross, and follow him. In these idyllic first moments, Jesus defines discipleship in its simplest terms, "Follow me."

Contemplate the brothers' surprising response to Jesus's offer. "Right away, they left their nets and followed him" (v. 20). They went *all in*, leaving family, friends, and vocation behind to follow wherever Christ might lead.

Continuing along the shore, they encounter James and John, the sons of Zebedee. Later, the two brothers will earn the nickname "the Sons of Thunder." Here and now, however, they meekly submit to Christ's call. Matthew does not record Zebedee's reaction to his children abandoning him with a pile of soggy, torn nets.

The pericope concludes with a summary of Jesus's early ministry, which includes teaching in the synagogues, proclaiming the kingdom's good news, and curing the sick. In the coming chapters, Matthew will add detail to Christ's Galilean itinerary.

Bringing the Text to Life

Matthew 4:12-23 provides an embarrassment of homiletical riches, and a preacher must choose between the dozen verses. The pericope provides enough material for several sermons, but let's focus on the call of the first disciples.

A document titled "A Simple Guide to Candidacy" describes the path to ordination for a United Methodist elder or deacon. The two-page flowchart lists eighteen discrete steps. A high school senior would require a minimum of ten years to complete the process.

We can make discipleship and ministry too complicated. By contrast and comparison, Jesus's call of Simon and Andrew contains two simple words, "Follow me." Christian disciples follow in Christ's footsteps. We do not control the itinerary or agenda, and trouble occurs when we try to walk beside or ahead of the Lord.

Years ago, I participated in a Honduran mission trip. I combine a Type-A personality with an OCD bent as a number one on the Enneagram! Therefore, I pestered the group leader, requesting details about the agenda. She repeatedly encouraged me to relax. I awoke the next day to find my watch's hour hand spinning frantically around the dial. I may be stubborn, but I am coachable! I threw away the watch and embraced the moment. Christians discover life-giving freedom when we let go and let God.

During the 1970s, the Lay Witness Movement thrived in The United Methodist Church. Lay teams spent weekends at host churches, sharing their personal testimonies. Perhaps pastors and/or laity can share their own call stories. If a congregation possesses the resources, create videos edited for time and content and share the testimonies on social media. Ask people to respond to two questions, "When was the *first* time you heard Jesus's call?" and "When was the *last* time you heard Jesus's call?"

For churches that have a children's time at the altar, play a game of "Follow the Leader" or "Simon Peter Says." (See what I did there?)

January 29, 2023–Fourth Sunday after the Epiphany

*Micah 6:1-8; **Psalm 15**; 1 Corinthians 1:18-31; Matthew 5:1-12*

Bill Burch

Preacher to Preacher Prayer

Almighty God, I enter your house and pulpit, a hypocrite preaching to hypocrites. Grant me the grace to proclaim your Word with integrity. May the act of preaching transform my life. Speak to me, through me, and despite me. Amen.

Commentary

Psalms 15–24 form a collection of complementary psalms with interwoven themes. Psalms 15 and 24 bookend the unit with liturgies for entry into the Jerusalem Temple. Their call-and-response pattern invites the faithful to worship in God's house.

Psalm 15 introduces the section by asking, "Who can live in your tent, Lord? Who can dwell on your holy mountain?" (v. 1). The parallelism of the two questions reinforces the worship leader's inquiry.

God's tent references the Tabernacle built by Moses in Exodus. The portable sanctuary contained the ark of the covenant, an incarnate reminder of God's presence. In 2 Samuel 6, King David moved the ark to his new capital city of Jerusalem. On this holy mountain, the Jews gathered to worship.

In response to the twin questions, the author lists the attributes of those who can enter into the Lord's presence. The list is both descriptive and aspirational. Throughout the Bible, God's people experience a tension between grace and works.

On the one hand, the holy attributes listed in Psalm 15 describe how worship converts the participants. God's grace transforms sinners into saints. In Romans 8:30, Paul delineates the process of sanctification, "Those who God decided in advance would be conformed to his Son, he also called. Those whom he called, he also made righteous. Those whom he made righteous, he also glorified."

On the other hand, the liturgy challenges worshippers to aspire to holier lives. Secure in the knowledge of divine grace and love, the faithful become the people God created them to be. Human effort partners with divine empowerment, resulting in transformed lives.

Naturally and supernaturally, the holy attributes of the faithful reflect the holy nature of the Lord. Humans who live and dwell in God's presence bear the fruit of divine holiness in thought, word, and deed.

The psalmist lists ten or more qualities of those who enter to worship. Some commentaries suggest the verses reflect the Ten Commandments; however, scholars perform hermeneutical gymnastics to make the case.

A preacher can approach verses 2-5 in two complementary ways. First, one can parse the psalm's phrases, focusing on each attribute. For example, what does it mean to live a life free of blame, to do what is right, and to speak the truth sincerely? Value exists in describing esoteric holiness in practical terms delineated by the psalm.

Second, one can treat verses 2-5 as a composite portrait of faithfulness. Like the fruit of the Spirit in Galatians 5:22-23, all of these characteristics grow organically in those who dwell in God's presence. We don't collect each attribute like a Boy Scout merit badge. In John 15, Jesus said that he is the vine and we are the branches. Those who abide in Christ bear much fruit. Apart from this life-giving relationship, we can do nothing.

The psalm concludes with the assurance, "Whoever does these things will never stumble" (v. 5). Other versions translate the last word to say *moved* or *shaken*. The author does not promise a problem-free life. However, God's people can depend upon a power beyond their own, which will sustain in this life and the life to come.

In Matthew 7:24-27, Jesus tells the parable of the two foundations. The story describes two people who build houses on bedrock and sand. When the rains fall and the storms surge, the home on bedrock survives, but the structure on sand collapses.

Jesus atypically begins the story with the punchline, "Everybody who hears these words of mine and puts them into practice is like a wise builder who built a house on bedrock" (Matt 7:24). The storms still rage; but those who build on a firm foundation are not moved.

Bringing the Text to Life

Today's lections provide an amazing breadth of homiletical material. Micah 6:8 challenges Israel "to do justice, embrace faithful love, and walk humbly with your God." Paul declares, "We preach Christ crucified" (1 Cor 1:23). Matthew 5:1-12 introduces the Sermon on the Mount with the Beatitudes.

Any of these passages provides abundant material for multiple sermons. This week's commentary focuses on Psalm 15, which highlights the theme of integrity embedded in all four passages.

Synonyms for integrity include soundness, honesty, unity, or oneness. From its root word, we get terms like "integral" (essential, complete), "integer" (whole number), and "integration" (various parts joined together into a united whole).

Persons of integrity exhibit a constancy of heart, soul, mind, and strength. The virtue connects profession and practice, word and deed, thought and action.

The opposite of integrity is hypocrisy. The word *hypocrite* comes from classic Greek drama. In ancient plays, actors ("hypokrites") wore masks to portray emotions. The word evolved to describe someone whose outward appearance and inward being do not match. Hypocrites say one thing but do another.

In 1936, the *Queen Mary* set sail as one of the largest cruise ships of the time. She survived four decades at sea, along with World War II. Following decommissioning, the *Queen Mary* docked at Long Beach, California, as a floating museum and hotel. During the conversion, cranes removed the three large smokestacks. Weakened by rust, sections of the funnels crumpled on the dock. Hypocrisy gives a semblance of substance that collapses under pressure.

For Christians, integrity is both gift and goal. God's justifying grace accepts us "as is." The Holy Spirit begins the process of sanctification. In today's lections, Micah, David, Paul, and Jesus sketch the faces of the faithful who embody integrity.

February 5, 2023–Fifth Sunday after the Epiphany

Isaiah 58:1-9a, (9b-12); Psalm 112:1-9 (10);
1 Corinthians 2:1-12 (13-16); *Matthew 5:13-20*

Bill Burch

Preacher to Preacher Prayer

Holy Spirit, humble me to preach Christ crucified. Inspire me to preach Christ crucified. Empower me to preach Christ crucified. Amen.

Commentary

The Apostle Paul first visited Corinth about 50 CE during his second missionary journey (Acts 18). The Corinthian Isthmus joins the Greek mainland with the Peloponnese Peninsula. The city's strategic location made it a vital hub for commerce and transportation in the Roman Empire. A diverse population, including large numbers of Romans and Jews, lived in the region.

As an evangelist and church planter, Paul relished the opportunity to preach the gospel in Corinth. After rejection in the local synagogue, the apostle preached to the Gentiles. During his eighteen-month tenure in the area, many joined the growing church. Paul wrote his first letter to the Corinthians several years later, responding to reported problems in the congregation.

In 1 Corinthians 2:1-2, Paul recalls his arrival in Corinth: "I didn't come preaching God's secrets to you like I was an expert in speech or wisdom. I had made up my mind not to think about anything else while I was with you except Jesus Christ, and to preach him as crucified."

Prior to his visit, Paul made an unsuccessful stop in Athens (Acts 17). Paul's sermon on Mars Hill attempted to co-opt Greek philosophy to explain the gospel; however, the homily underwhelmed his audience. Many ridiculed the message while a few wanted to hear more.

Perhaps the failure in Athens shaped Paul's ministry in Corinth. In 1 Corinthians 1:22-23, Paul writes, "Jews ask for signs, and Greeks look for wisdom, but we preach Christ crucified, which is a scandal to Jews and foolishness to Gentiles." Paul resolves to focus on the central message of the gospel: the crucifixion (and resurrection) of Jesus Christ.

Paul claims he preached to the Corinthians with "weakness, fear, and a lot of shaking" (1 Cor 2:3). Although some might dismiss the statement as false humility, Paul often downplays his public rhetoric and physical appearance. However, "a demonstration of the Spirit and of power" accompanied the sermons (1 Cor 2:4). Later, Paul reflects, "But we have this treasure in clay pots so that the awesome power belongs to God and doesn't come from us" (2 Cor 4:7).

Paul writes in verse 6, "What we say is wisdom to people who are mature." Scholars note a twofold division of the Christian message in the New Testament. Kerygma entails the evangelical proclamation of the gospel to nonbelievers. Didache describes the instruction and edification of believers. The latter is the "wisdom" that Paul references.

Compare and contrast the New Testament ideas of Kerygma and Didache to John Wesley's understanding of prevenient, justifying, and sanctifying grace. Like a Venn diagram, the theological concepts express distinctive but overlapping realities.

In the remainder of the pericope, the apostle divides humanity into two groups. The spirit-filled Christian receives God's wisdom and cultivates the mind of Christ. The unspiritual person embraces worldly knowledge and nurtures a mind of carnality.

Paul does not describe a gnosis or secret knowledge available to advanced initiates of the faith. Instead, the apostle states that only the Holy Spirit reveals spiritual truths. Spirit-filled Christians get it, and worldly people cannot.

Paul concludes the chapter, "But we have the mind of Christ" (1 Cor 2:16). Like the entirety of the Christian experience, possessing Christ's mind is both gift and goal. The indwelling power of the Holy Spirit grants a new perspective and understanding. The process of sanctification lasts a lifetime. In Romans 12:2, Paul writes, "Don't be conformed to the patterns of this world, but be transformed by the renewing of your minds so that you can figure out what God's will is—what is good and pleasing and mature."

Bringing the Text to Life

When I pass a church with "Corinth" in the name, I wonder if anyone read the Bible before naming the church! The Corinthian congregation's problems inspired Paul's multiple letters.

Paul evangelized the Mediterranean basin and wrote almost one-third of the New Testament. However, he spoke with fear and trembling to the Corinthians. The Holy Spirit calls contemporary clergy to present themselves as workers approved by God (2 Tim 2:15); however, preachers are earthen vessels containing heavenly treasure. God speaks to, through, and despite the person behind the pulpit.

A spirit of humility focuses on Christ crucified rather than human eloquence. I recall preaching for a Presbyterian pastor who was ill on Christmas Eve. Behind the pulpit, a prominent sign exclaimed, "Sir, we would see Jesus" (see John 12:21). I often think of this quote before a sermon. Every pastor has more than a little pride in preaching, but the Spirit nudges us aside so that others can see Jesus.

The Holy Spirit also intervenes between the spoken and heard Word. Some days I limp away from the pulpit, disappointed in my poor performance. Inevitably, saints will claim it was the best sermon they've ever heard! On other occasions, people quote a meaningful part of the sermon that I never spoke.

As a well-meaning parishioner said in my first church, "Don't worry, son, if God could use an ass to speak to Balaam, then the Lord can use you to speak to us!" (Num 22:20-39).

Paul divides the world into two types of people: the spiritual and the worldly. Only the former understands God's wisdom. A church member wore a T-shirt to Bible study that states it well, "You either get it or you don't!"

Finally, the cruciform or cross-shaped life cultivates the mind of Christ. This transforms the way Christians see the world. In tech terms, a spirit-filled perspective enables us to experience a faith-augmented reality that distinguishes between the temporal and eternal.

February 12, 2023–Sixth Sunday after the Epiphany

Deuteronomy 30:15-20; Psalm 119:1-8; 1 Corinthians 3:1-9;
Matthew 5:21-37

Robin Wilson

Preacher to Preacher Prayer

Almighty God, the gifts of the magi have long been forgotten since Epiphany Sunday. Help us to continue to bring you our best as we prepare to preach to your people. May we choose a life of love and obedience as we offer you our best this day. In the name of the one who came to save the world, Jesus the Christ, we pray. Amen.

Commentary

The people of God are almost there. After decades of wandering, losing hope, regaining hope, complaining about manna, wanting to turn back, fighting with enemy armies, and so much more, they are almost to the land that was promised to them by God. This new generation has been brought up out of Egypt and in the wilderness, hearing the instruction of Moses and the stories of their ancestors. They have also heard about this land that God will give them, and that day is so close. The excitement and energy must be palpable, as would be anxiety and fear of the unknown. After all, this is a huge change for our wanderers. The thought of a home, a place that is theirs . . . it has just been a dream for so long.

Moses has led them along this journey, and at this point, he is an old man. Just prior to this passage, the people have heard of God's history of faithfulness to God's people. They have been given the Ten Commandments, heard the case laws, and been subject to a lengthy discussion of the penalties and curses for disobedience (Deut 28:15-68) and blessings for obedience to the laws (Deut 28:1-14). So, at this point, as the people are primed with instruction on how to live in obedience in response to God, Moses shares his wisdom about the next steps in their journey.

Verse 16 summarizes how they are to live in response to their God. "If you obey the LORD your God's commandments that I'm commanding you right now by loving the Lᴏʀᴅ your God, by walking in his ways, and by keeping his commandments, his regulations, and his case laws, then you will live and thrive, and the Lᴏʀᴅ your God will bless you in the land you are entering to possess." All they must do to receive God's blessings in this new land is summed up here. Verses 19-20 spell out to the community that it is still their decision to choose this abundant grounded life in their new homeland.

Wander in the wilderness or have a home. Receive blessings or penalties and curses. That's where Moses leaves them at the end of this pericope. As we hear the scripture read, the new hearer unfamiliar with the story could be on the edge of the pew awaiting the decision of the people to live a life of love, obedience, and blessing . . . or a life of drifting, curses, and wilderness wandering.

Bringing the Text to Life

Old-man Moses must have looked with love and wisdom at his people as they approached the promised land. He devoted everything he had to listening to God and leading God's people through this time of wilderness wandering. Sometimes he made good decisions; other times, he didn't. But throughout all of his leading, he had to have loved these people. And he knew enough to share these words of wisdom with them as they approached their destination.

Parents, educators, and others who have had a hand in molding and shaping lives will relate to this Moses, who has led with all of his flaws by the grace of God. And as they approach what will be the end of his time with them, his need to share the most important wisdom he has is understandable to so many. You might share words from famous graduation speeches. Talk about the tender words you have heard in your life and ministry of those who wanted to share their wisdom. Talk about a teacher, a parent, a friend who spoke deep wisdom into your life about how to choose to live a life of love and blessing.

Invite the congregation to remember the wilderness they have been through as a community. Remind them to remember what it was like after the tornado, the hurricane, the pandemic, the fire, or another applicable crisis in their life together. That community had a choice to make: to come together in love and obedience, knowing that God would not forsake them to a lifetime of that wilderness, or turn their backs to the blessings God had provided for them together. After all, this text is not written to those who already are in covenant with God, so that they will step into the land and blessings that God has promised. Preach the word to the congregation that they have already learned of God's faithfulness in history and in their life together; they get to decide together to live that life of love and obedience together. As they look at living in love and obedience, invite your congregation to see that part of that includes passing along the wisdom that they accumulate in their lives, just like Moses.

As this is two Sundays before Lent, this is a great place to stress your Lenten discipleship and mission opportunities as a place to commit to growing in love and obedience to God. Be well-prepared to offer a way for your congregation to grow together and move as a community closer to God. Additionally, invite them to reflect on what wisdom they would love to share with their students, grandchildren, or others in their lives. Perhaps include note cards and envelopes with time in the service for people to write a brief word as they are moved to do.

The words from Dr. Martin Luther King Jr.'s last speech in Memphis would be interesting to incorporate in your closing. As he addressed those in Memphis, while working with the sanitation workers in that city, he closed his speech with these words, "I'm not fearing any man. Mine eyes have seen the glory of the coming of the Lord."[1]

February 19, 2023– Transfiguration Sunday

Exodus 24:12-18; Psalm 2 or Psalm 99; 2 Peter 1:16-21;
Matthew 17:1-9

Robin Wilson

Preacher to Preacher Prayer

Radiant God, you are constantly revealing more of yourself to us. This Transfiguration Sunday, shine into our world, and may we have the wherewithal to listen as you lead us. Close our mouths and open our hearts this day. In the name of the one who surprises us with the fullness of his compassion, Jesus the Christ. Amen.

Commentary

Poor Peter. He does not know what to expect when Jesus leads him and the other two followers to the top of a mountain . . . a high mountain, Matthew tells us. Mountains are significant, of course. That's where Abraham is to sacrifice his son Isaac (Gen 22:2), Moses gets the Ten Commandments (Exod 20; Num 3:10), Elijah meets the Baal prophets (1 Kgs 18:17-46), Jesus preaches his Sermon on the Mount (Matt 5:1), just to name a few. All of these are wonderful stories, which would have been familiar to disciples of Jesus who were Jewish and who kept up with his preaching schedule. But the last time the author of Matthew mentions a high mountain, it was when Jesus was taken there and tempted by the devil after Jesus's baptism (Matt 4:8). Who knows what Peter and the others thought they would encounter going up this high mountain with Jesus.

When Jesus was transformed and talking to Moses and Elijah, heavyweights with the Law and the Prophets, it is Peter who speaks. His response to this shining Jesus is hard to interpret. Does he want to preserve the moment by building a shrine to remember this moment, like we get out our iPhones today to record important moments in our lives? Does he not know what to say but just babbles? Is he frightened, not knowing what this moment means?

The scripture tells us that the cloud came "while [Peter] was still speaking" (Matt 17:5). Isn't that wonderful, that God was moving while the others didn't know what to do? The words from the cloud confirming the identity of Jesus as God's Son inspired awe and fear, appropriately. The last words from the cloud were the command, "Listen to him" (Matt 17:5). It was impossible for them to listen while they were talking. God moved during their words and almost spoke over Peter.

As they descended the mountain, the instructions from Jesus also involved not talking. They were to tell no one about the vision until after the Resurrection. So the instructions they received were to listen to Jesus and keep their mouths shut until more was revealed. What excellent instructions for us as we try and make sense of the sacred moments in our lives.

Bringing the Text to Life

How often do we ruin moments that are sacred and holy with our desire to capture the memory? Tell about weddings you have seen ruined by photographers or cell phones. Ask your congregation if they have had their view blocked at a recital, sporting event, or concert by an overzealous fan with a cell phone or camera trying to record the event for posterity. You might remark that you knew the quality of the video or picture would never be as good as the live event.

How much we miss in this culture when we do not allow ourselves moments of silence and stillness in the face of the profound. Many in our congregations will relate to Peter's reaction, for they may have messed up such a moment in their own lives. My own example is after my husband and I recessed after our wedding, I immediately went into task mode and began the march to get pictures made. When I stopped and looked at my new husband, I could see how awestruck he was by the idea that we joined our lives and knelt in prayer asking God to bless us in our covenant together. It was a holy moment where he experienced God and was in awe-filled silence, while I was rushing to take a picture and record the moment.

Point out that even though Peter kept talking and over-functioning, God enveloped the disciples in a cloud and interrupted them by revealing more about Jesus. Even when we are busy and over-functioning, without the wisdom to listen and be still, God acts for our good anyway. This will serve to remind the congregation that the transfiguration was about God, not about Peter.

Sometimes we forget that God acts for our good, even when we don't have the good sense to be quiet. Some biblical examples of Mary the mother of Jesus, who "treasured all these words and pondered them in her heart" (Luke 2:19) or Martha's sister, Mary, who sat at Jesus's feet and listened to his teachings, would be good to note as examples of those who listened to God. They stopped, listened, and responded humbly throughout their lives for God.

February 22, 2023– Ash Wednesday

Joel 2:1-2, 12-17 or Isaiah 58:1-12; Psalm 51:1-17;
*2 Corinthians 5:20b-6:10; **Matthew 6:1-6, 16-21***

Robin Wilson

Preacher to Preacher Prayer

God of light and ashes, we marvel at our fast journey from the mountaintop with you, Moses, and Elijah to the time of dust and ashes of this day. Just as we saw your glory in the light of your transfiguration, may we see your light in the ashes we wear on this day. In the name of the only one who can save us from our sins and ourselves, Jesus the Christ. Amen.

Commentary

Last Sunday, we celebrated the wonder of Jesus, as his transfiguration revealed and confirmed his identity as the Son of God. As his face shone bright, we recognized with Peter, James, and John that Jesus was greater than we could ever imagine. And now on Ash Wednesday, in the glow of the one who was sinless, we begin to take stock of ourselves in comparison, admitting how much we are in need of a savior.

Matthew 6 is in the middle of Jesus's Sermon on the Mount. Our passage for Ash Wednesday has Jesus preaching about how authentically "practicing your religion" is not about drawing attention to the act of piety. The series of instructions that Jesus gives about how to give to the poor (Matt 6:2-4), how to pray (Matt 6:5-6), and how to fast (Matt 6:16-18) all have the same themes. First, it assumes that the hearers are already participating in the activity. Matthew's Gospel is aimed at those Jews, not Gentiles, so they would be familiar with these practices of faith. Thus, the word is not *if* but *when*. This sermon is not meant to goad people into giving to the poor, praying, or fasting; it is instead intended to check the motive and behavior of those who already seek to be faithful in practice. On Ash Wednesday, those who attend this mid-week service are often the faithful churchgoers who might need to be likewise reminded of the practices Jesus assumes that the faithful are already engaging in.

Second, Jesus is very clear that the practicing of religion is not intended to impress others with acts of piety or draw attention. Instead, it is clear that the acts that are a part of faithful living are done humbly in response to God. This can be difficult to communicate in a culture that measures its worth in social media likes and followers. Perhaps that is an honest struggle to admit to the congregation. Churches fall into the same trap—posting their mission-trip photos, youth group activities, and well-kept worship venues. It is an honest struggle to discern whether our motives are to be salt and light, as Jesus just preached about in Matthew 5:13-16, or to draw attention and admiration to ourselves as pious and faithful.

The last part of this pericope does not begin with the word *when*. Instead, the imperative command to "stop" seems more forceful. It implies that the people had been looking to themselves and things of the world to benefit them. Jesus tells them to stop and instead collect treasures in heaven. Perhaps these treasures are found when the previously named practices (fasting, praying, sharing with the poor) and all the practices of faith are done with proper motive and not for show.

Bringing the Text to Life

Considering our human frailty and bent to sinning, it is easy to take pride in wearing the ashes of Ash Wednesday. After all, when we are marked with the ashes, we walk around for the rest of our day with the sign of the cross. We are far from praying in secret, fasting and washing our faces, or sharing with others in secret. What a good moment to talk about what the ashes actually signify. The ashes are not a symbol of piety but of our human sinfulness, brokenness, and humility. Yet as they are formed into the shape of the cross, it humbly shows that something so ugly as ashes can be used by God to begin to focus the world onto the cross. These cross-shaped ashes tell the world that we submit to the only one who can save the world.

Nathaniel Hawthorne's 1850 novel *The Scarlet Letter* details the story of Hester Prynne, who is convicted of adultery and forced to wear a scarlet *A* to stigmatize and humiliate her in public. It is a tragic tale of shame and pain. Contrast this with the ashes we wear on Ash Wednesday. We wear them for a night to mark the beginning of this season of Lent, this time for repentance and reflection upon our desperate need of a savior. Hester had to continue to wear her mark; we will wash ours off. But through our time of Lent, we carry that need to refocus on the acts of our faith (prayer, fasting, sharing with the poor) with humility and love. We do so knowing that it is through faithful living that we can truly be a city on a hill and salt of the earth. God's light shines through the cross of Christ in each moment as we live faithfully. That is how we shine the message of Jesus through the times of ashes of life. We are not stained by sin or ashes, we are not humiliated by displaying them forever, but neither are we glorified by wearing them either. It all is a reminder of who Jesus is and what he accomplishes for us and, indeed, through us.

February 26, 2023–First Sunday in Lent

*Genesis 2:15-17; 3:1-7; Psalm 32; Romans 5:12-19; **Matthew 4:1-11***

Susan Gray

Preacher to Preacher Prayer

O God of our baptism and God of the wilderness, lead us both into the waters of new life and the wilderness of barren truth this Lenten season. May your Spirit be a compass for us as we lead your people through Lent. We await you with anticipated expectation. We trust that you will show up in the most surprising ways and expand our capacity for love. Amen.

Commentary

For centuries, scholars have mined this rich text for meaning and truth, offering many possible sermon themes in the process. The parallels between Jesus's forty days in the wilderness and the Israelites' forty years in the desert leap out of the text with obvious clarity.

Before Jesus had done a single thing for God, God's delight in Jesus was made known, "This is my Son, the Beloved, with whom I am well pleased" (Matt 3:17 NRSV). Then Jesus was led by the Spirit into the wilderness. The wilderness has long been understood as a place of preparation and waiting for God's leading. It is a place where things like trust and reliance on God are learned.

When I moved to Indiana with my husband and three school-aged children in the winter of 2000, I had no idea that I was moving into a time of spiritual wilderness. The lessons I learned during that time have been invaluable to me not only as a follower of Christ, but as a spiritual leader of the church. One of the lessons I learned is that who I am to God is far greater than what I do for God. I learned that God's church could run just fine without me. Serving God is a privilege, not a God-given right.

There are many lessons to be learned in the wilderness. Perhaps the first lesson comes in examining the question, "How did Jesus have the ability to overcome the temptation he encountered?" The answer may come down to Jesus's own relationship with God. As a Jewish male, Jesus would be very aware of the struggles and pain the Hebrew people faced in their own wilderness experience. Jesus, like Israel, learned to trust in God to provide all he would need to endure.

For Israel, learning to trust God became essential to their survival. Israel had long been vulnerable to the ancient Near East superpowers and was beleaguered from centuries of oppression. In the time of this text, they were finding themselves being crushed and oppressed by the Roman superpower who had a presence in nearly every city. The Romans were heavily taxing the Israelites and crushing any hope of resistance. Once again, the Israelites were a devastated people looking to God for help. Jesus was there to help. At the end of Jesus's forty days, when his body was weak from hunger and isolation, temptation came at him when his humanity was most vulnerable.

The first temptation came to Jesus through his physical need of hunger. He hadn't eaten in forty days. Yet, Jesus's response claims a trust in God to fulfill a deeper need than physical hunger and one that will fill his life with something mere bread could never fill. The second temptation occurred at the pinnacle of the temple in Jerusalem. Here, Jesus could have caved and performed a miracle. However, this would set people up to fail in their faith. What would happen if God didn't step in and perform on command the next time a crisis emerged? Would they still trust in God if God didn't respond the way they wanted? This kind of faith is more focused on what God can do for us rather than who we are to God. Finally, the last miracle occurred when Jesus was offered all the kingdoms of the world and this temptation was seemingly and swiftly dismissed by Jesus.

Jesus put his relationship with the God of love over a relationship with power and prestige. Jesus would go on to perform many miracles of power but not for the purpose of show. Rather, Jesus used his power for the purpose of sharing God's love and compassion with God's people. He would feed five thousand with five loaves of bread and two fish. He would make people walk. He would restore sight to the blind. Jesus was not afraid to use his power, but he used his power to help others—not to gain position for himself.

Jesus answered every temptation in a way that did not betray his relationship with God, or his mission and ministry. After spending forty days in the wilderness, surely Jesus experienced the nearness of the Holy Spirit. Jesus knew with absolute clarity it was the love of God that sustained the part of him that was human during his struggle. He grew in trust that it would be the love of God that would provide him with the strength to endure his upcoming ministry.

Bringing the Text to Life

For Jesus, to give in to immediate satisfaction of physical pleasure or earthly power would be to betray the greater power he had in his own relationship of love with God. When we find our lives in times of struggle, hardship, or temptation, we can lean into our relationship with God and trust God to see us through. For example, what I learned during my time in the wilderness is that God cares more about who I am than what I do. This can be the struggle for followers of Jesus. We are so trained to be doing for God that we forget to take time to be with God. Sometimes, God may just want us to sit or take a walk. Sometimes, God wants to lead us into the wilderness to speak to our hearts. Encourage your people to follow the Spirit into the wilderness of Lent.

March 5, 2023–Second Sunday in Lent

Genesis 12:1-4a; Psalm 121; Romans 4:1-5, 13-17; **John 3:1-17**

Susan Gray

Preacher to Preacher Prayer

Eternal God of our salvation, on this second Sunday of Lent may we, the leaders of your church, be like Nicodemus and seek first a deeper truth from you. Help us to lead your people into a deeper understanding of who you are so that we may be made new again. Amen.

Commentary

The story of Jesus's conversation with Nicodemus is unique to the Gospel of John. The central theme in the conversation between Nicodemus and Jesus is the question of the kingdom of God and the means of entrance into it. Nicodemus in not named in the Synoptic Gospels. He was a Pharisee and a member of the Sanhedrin. We often think of the Jewish men holding such positions as being hostile toward Jesus. Yet, here we have someone who seemingly appears to be a seeker of the truth. Did Jesus say something that rang as truth to Nicodemus? While he may have been a seeker, he was cautious as to how he looked for truth as demonstrated by seeking Jesus out in the dark of night. Perhaps Nicodemus was being extremely careful not to be seen with Jesus. Perhaps he was unable to sleep because his mind was working overtime trying to process Jesus's teachings. Either way, into the night he went to see Jesus. Nicodemus begins the conversation acknowledging Jesus as a teacher who came from God because of the miraculous signs he has performed. Next, one of the most unusual theological conversations unfolds.

Jesus responds to Nicodemus that "unless someone is born of water and the Spirit, it's not possible to enter God's kingdom" (John 3:5). This one sentence has been followed with centuries of theological scholarship resulting in multiple conclusions. In college, I once had a classmate follow me down the street repeatedly asking, "But have you been born again?" At the age of nineteen, I wasn't sure what answer he wanted from me so I simply turned and said, "I've been baptized." Yet, he kept pursuit with the same voice of fear questioning me. I knew my soul was at peace with God. I wasn't so sure about my classmate's.

So, how do we preach this passage? We know it was never recorded that Jesus made an old person young again while on earth. This leaves the assumption that Jesus is not speaking about a physical reality but, rather, a spiritual reality. We are born from water at our human birth and we are born of Spirit at our spiritual birth. When we awaken to our understanding that God makes all things new, we are born anew.

We see other places in scripture where authors write of the importance of God making all things new. God gives the house of Israel a new birth when He says, "I will give you a new heart and put a new spirit in you. I will remove your stony heart from your body and replace it with a living one" (Ezek 36:26). On an individual level, the psalmist seeks to be made new in Psalm 51:10, "Create a clean heart for me, God; put a new, faithful spirit deep inside me!" Seeking a new start with God is nothing new for the people of God and it was not new for Nicodemus.

We will never know how God makes all things new, but, in this text, we learn God will make things new through Jesus. Jesus continues the conversation by inviting Nicodemus into a deeper understanding of the kingdom of God. He reminds Nicodemus of the story of Moses and the serpent. When Israel was bitter and complaining about God, Moses lifted up a bronze snake on a pole so that the people of Israel could see it, be forgiven, and live. In the same way, Jesus is lifted up on the cross so that we might see him, receive forgiveness, and live. When we see the humility of Christ on the cross we see a stark contrast between the love of God and the degradation of humanity.

God steps into our broken humanity and overcomes our sin with God's love. When we receive God's love, we begin to change—not physically, but spiritually. God's love in us opens us to see the world differently, too. Our hearts are changed and we are simply never the same.

Bringing the Text to Life

Nicodemus is seen one more time in the Gospel of John when he accompanies Joseph of Arimathea to ask for Jesus's body after he was crucified. Once more, we see Nicodemus stepping out of his comfort zone for Jesus. Peter is off betraying Jesus; others are hidden and scared. What propels Nicodemus to risk the dangerous fate that would surely await him if he is seen wanting to help Jesus—even a dead Jesus?

Could it be that, by the end, Nicodemus understood Jesus's teaching? Did he now understand that eternal life is not about a destination, but about a way of life both here and now and continues throughout eternity? Jesus did not so much show us a roadmap to get to heaven when we die. Rather, Jesus gave us a roadmap to find heaven while we live. This understanding shifts the conversation of salvation from fear based to love based.

Salvation (eternal life) begins when we place our faith in Jesus and allow the love of God into our lives. When we receive God's love as a response to our brokenness, we are saved. It's not about the water or the flesh; it is about God's love. God's love makes us new. God's love can make new all that is broken in our life: our marriages, relationships, or jobs. Whatever is broken, God can and will make new. Invite people to give over to God what is broken and allow the Spirit of God to do a new thing.

March 12, 2023–Third Sunday in Lent

Exodus 17:1-7; Psalm 95; Romans 5:1-11; John 4:5-42

Susan Gray

Preacher to Preacher Prayer

O God of the wilderness, from a rock you offered your thirsty people a drink of water. Give to us, your leaders, a fresh drink today of Living Water so that we may be refreshed through your life once more.

Commentary

The wilderness theme emerges again in this Lenten text. This time it is seen through the story of the Israelites and Moses as they wander through the desert. The Israelites are tired, hungry, and thirsty. This is not a good combination. Parents with children on vacation already know this. In our family, we used to call it hangry-time. The Israelites are hangry on steroids. So, they did what many of us do. They begin to question the wisdom of the authority figure in charge. They question Moses's leadership skills. They tell him to produce water to show them that he is indeed God's leader. The previous miracles were not enough. They needed proof again.

The wilderness is an interesting and complex place. It is not only a barren geographical location, it can also be a mental location. It can be a way of thinking. The Israelites believe they are God's chosen people, and yet, they don't understand God's ways. Not understanding something makes it easy for one to doubt. Chaos and confusion began to set into their way of thinking. For anyone who has been in a wilderness time in their lives, they have probably discovered what Israel was discovering. Real life and perceived life can become very confusing. Trusting in God while not understanding the ways of God can make people question their faith. The oasis ahead often ends up being more dust in the sand or more salt in the wound rather than a refreshing drink of water.

Doubt can impinge on thinking when people feel unable to tell real life from perceived life. Wandering in the wilderness fatigued mentally, spiritually, and emotionally can cause the most faithful to begin to question. We know this to be true from Mother Teresa. Once this level of fatigue happens, it isn't surprising that bitterness, complaining, and confrontation follow. This happened for Israel at the place called Massah/Meribah, which means "divine test" or "putting God to the proof." They wanted Yahweh to show them who God was by doing what they wanted God to do for them. If they were to continue to place their faith in God, then God needed to show them something they could believe.

When this demand is placed on God, faith becomes something more based on what God can do for humans than on who God is to humans. Humans complaining to God is not new, rather, it is predictable. We rely on what our eyes can see. In the beginning of humanity, it was necessary for survival. Wild animals are dangerous. If you see a wild animal, you avoid it or it might kill you. Yet, a deeper life with God requires something we can't see with our eyes. It requires believing in what we can't see. In our culture we often hear "seeing is believing." Yet, with God, believing is seeing. To see the things of God, we must first believe and trust in God.

This kind of faith allows us to hang on to our faith in the wilderness and chaotic times. It allows us to trust in God even when we don't understand where God is or see what God is doing. God's promise to God's people is that God will satisfy them abundantly. This means we don't always get what we want. Jesus fed five thousand people with five loaves of bread and two fish. The scripture says the people "had plenty to eat" (John 6:12). Yet, they hungered for more the next day. They followed Jesus to the other side asking him for more bread. He told them he was "the bread of life" and when we eat this bread, we will hunger no more (John 6:35). The true Bread of Life satisfies us when we can't satisfy ourselves. It may not always be what we want when we want, but it will always be what we need.

Bringing the Text to Life

One of the takeaways from this passage is that it is OK to cry and complain to God. God not only heard the complaints of the Israelite community but God also responded and gave them what they needed. In the same way, we can have confidence that when we cry out to God, God will hear us and respond to us as well. The wilderness is a place to cry out to God.

God will meet us in the wilderness. Although we may feel all alone, God will not leave us alone or abandon us. God will provide manna and water when we are hungry and thirsty. However, this requires us showing up. It requires us engaging with God even when we are fatigued from life. How often we make excuses or can't find time in our busy schedules to carve out time for God—even if it's time spent complaining to God. The people were not condemned for asking for water, they were chastised for demanding proof of deity from God.

Lent is a season of wrestling with our own inner life and our life of faith. Invite people to find their place in this story. Are you in a barren land this Lent? Are you the one with the stick to help another who is thirsty find water? Are you a leader who is watching everything unfold? How is the rock there for you? Is the rock for you to sit on and rest a while? Is the rock a place for you to cry out to God or a place for you to sit and have a glass of water with God? Invite people to meet God in the wilderness and see where and how God shows up.

March 19, 2023–Fourth Sunday in Lent

*1 Samuel 16:1-13; **Psalm 23**; Ephesians 5:8-14; John 9:1-41*

DJ del Rosario

Preacher to Preacher Prayer

Holy One, in every season there is new life and crossing the threshold to eternity. Death comes at any time, for anyone. Open my heart and whole self to the guidance of your Holy Spirit to experience the gift of life, death, and everything in between. Help me to imagine the flock of your community I serve to share your words and no other. Amen.

Commentary

> Surely your goodness and love will follow me all the days of my life,
> and I will dwell in the house of the LORD forever. —Psalm 23:6 NIV

Psalm 23 is one of the more familiar passages of scripture known throughout the world. In the music world, Tupac Shakur referenced the psalm in his song "So Many Tears," and Kanye West refers to the "valley of the shadow of death" in his famous song "Jesus Walks." While Psalm 23 is often interpreted as a song trusting Yahweh, rappers such as Tupac and Kanye use these verses from the viewpoint of sadness and lament. In James Cameron's epic movie *Titanic*, a priest recites Psalm 23 while the great ship is sinking. After the terrorist attacks on 9/11, President George Bush read the famous words from the psalmist when he addressed a nation in shock and mourning. Chances are that if you read even scant parts of this psalm, people will understand the reference overall.

One challenge of this chapter is to bring a fresh and new perspective on something so familiar. One approach you can take as the preacher is to address familiar cultural references of Psalm 23. I'll leave it to your discretion whether mentioning Kanye West or movies like *Titanic* is best. There are other ways to engage this passage of scripture as well. As you prepare to preach, how have you employed this psalm of David in your experience?

The temptation of reading the psalmist is often to focus on the final days of a person's life. One can't help thinking of memorials and times of sadness when this passage is read aloud. Philip Keller, author of "A Shepherd looks at Psalm 23," writes, "It must be kept in mind always, that the Psalmist, writing from the standpoint of a sheep, is reflecting and recounting the full round of the year's activities for the flock."[1] Shifting the perspective of how the reader views and interprets this passage can open a menagerie of new viewpoints.

What are some of the viewpoints that you can offer as the preacher to broaden the community's understanding of this psalm? You can paint a picture of the shepherd David writing this as a prayer to God as he watches over his sheep day and night. It's also possible to read this envisioning the multitude of times these sacred words have been read over history, from plagues and pandemics to times of grief and sorrow. Priests and people employ David's prayer time and time again. How is Yahweh calling you to share these familiar words in a life-giving way?

Bringing the Text to Life

There are many ways that you can help to bring this text to life. While you preach, you can offer sheets of paper and invite the community to write words or phrases that impact their hearts. Writing isn't the only way to artistically interpret this passage and your subsequent sermon. The community can also be invited to draw imagery that comes to mind as they listen to these verses read aloud. Find creative ways for people to share their words and drawings with others. Using social media is also an option. A low-tech alternative is to have folks pin their drawings on a wall, thereby creating a mosaic of experiences. Use the litany of responses as a way to invite the community to experience the movement of the Holy Spirit.

As the preacher, you can invite folks to rewrite Psalm 23 by interpreting the meaning in their lives and with modern-day imagery. Who is a modern-day version of a shepherd in your community? How do the people in your life address death and loss? Other questions you can use for reflection might be, How will you spend your life? How will the time you spend each day reflect what you love most?

March 25/26, 2023– Annunciation of the Lord/ Fifth Sunday in Lent

Isaiah 7:10-14; Psalm 45 or Psalm 40:5-10; Hebrews 10:4-10;
Luke 1:26-38
Ezekiel 37:1-14; Psalm 130; Romans 8:6-11; John 11:1-45

DJ del Rosario

Preacher to Preacher Prayer

Loving One, as we dive deeper into this season of Lent, prepare my heart and those of the people I serve to receive your word. Help me to see beyond a valley of dry bones. Teach me to invite your people to wrestle with the Hebrew Scripture and the gospel message with honesty and hope.

Commentary

This week you get a two-for-one day of remembrance. Not only do you get to focus on the Fifth Sunday of Lent, you also get to address the Annunciation of the Lord. The Annunciation of the Lord marks the visit of the angel Gabriel to the Virgin Mary. Within the orthodox Christian calendar, March 25 is marked as the day to remember this sacred encounter.

Beginning with Ezekiel 37, this passage focuses on the treatable and curable impurities the Hebrew people faced.[2] The Hebrew Scriptures have many rituals for washing and clean water. The essence of these cleaning rituals is to allow unclean persons to be reconnected back into sacred community. The prophet Ezekiel is writing about the people of Israel becoming bonded back into a whole and healthy relationship with God.

It's important to note that in Ezekiel, the Hebrew people are not required to do anything. Contrast this with the book of Leviticus that often requires confession and true repentance (Lev 26:40-45). In Ezekiel's passage, it's about God's gracious action and not the people's actions or inactions.[3] The prophet Ezekiel's words are a somber reminder that there are very few things happening in our world that are really in our control.

In a time of immediate news coverage, we are saturated with so much news, we often don't know what or whom to trust. We live in a world right now where there are so many over-the-top tweets, quotes, and misinformation being tossed about that it can be difficult to know what information to trust. In a time when people in power seemingly ask us to choose sides rather than drive toward unity, this just feels wrong in every sense. Those who are in nondominant culture or who have been marginalized have experienced what it's like to struggle to be heard, to be seen, to be valued. Living as a nondominant person is by definition a struggle when the cards are systematically stacked against you.

This type of work takes grit. It's not the easy path. But it is the path we are all on. Angela Duckworth is a distinguished professor of psychology at the University of Pennsylvania. She wrote a great book titled *Grit: The Power of Passion and Perseverance*. In it she wrote, "To be gritty is to keep putting one foot in front of the other. To be gritty is to hold fast to an interesting and purposeful goal. To be gritty is to invest, day after week after year, in challenging practice. To be gritty is to fall down seven times, and rise eight."[4] Following Jesus isn't about an easy life, or getting past our struggles, bad habits, addictions, depression, the power of positive thinking, or any other cliché that tempts us to believe all will be well as long as we find that silver bullet for all of life problems.

Shifting gears, let's focus on the Annunciation of the Lord. There are many ways you can invite the community to wrestle with this passage. As you begin your studies and reflection, what about this passage is bringing you hope? Are there aspects of the angel's encounter with Mary that are troublesome?

Considering that we live in a #MeToo time where women are given more benefit of the doubt than in the past few decades, how do we engage this passage through a modern-day lens? Don't shy away from challenging aspects of this passage. For example, why did the Angel of the Lord tell young Mary that she was pregnant? How would this passage be different if Mary were given a choice? Throughout history, we often lift up Mary's wise and sacred response. Could she have doubted or struggled? How might this passage be different from a modern-day perspective?

Bringing the Text to Life

Our past shapes us today and becomes a foundation for how we act in our future. It's easier to name our past failures and struggles rather than present ones. But, church can't be a place just for people who have things figured out, or for people who once struggled and are no longer struggling. Following Jesus can't just be about putting our best foot forward.

As you preach, remember that we all have a story. Some of our stories are ones we love and hold on to, while others are stories that cling to us like the smell of cigarette smoke. As you write your sermon, picture those who struggle in your community—some with cancer, others with different illnesses. Some struggle with addictions that get the better of us on more days than we would like to share. From alcohol, to things we find online, to relationships, depression—the list can go on. Still, others in our communities are struggling with the state of our families, our nation, and the world. How have your people struggled and celebrated together?

April 2, 2023–Palm/Passion Sunday

Psalm 118:1-2, 19-29; **Matthew 21:1-11**
Isaiah 50:4-9a; Psalm 31:9-16; **Philippians 2:5-11**; *Matthew 26:14–27:66 or Matthew 27:11-54*

DJ del Rosario

Preacher to Preacher Prayer

Lord, prepare our hearts to leave our expectations at the threshold of your kin-dom. Teach me to listen to the cry of those voices who are often unheard. Just as you defied expectations on Palm/Passion Sunday, defy our expectations for what this Sunday can be.

Commentary

Whether you choose to focus on Palm Sunday or Passion Sunday, the purpose of this liturgical Sunday is to remember the mission of the church. Disciples strive to live by the two great commands that Jesus gave us: to love God with all our heart, soul, minds and strength; and to love our neighbor as we love ourselves.

In all four Gospel accounts, there are stories of crowds that gathered around Jesus as he entered Jerusalem. In Matthew 21 and Mark 11, Jesus is greeted by crowds that are large—and nameless. Matthew focuses on the energy surrounding Jesus's entry: as the city asked, "Who is this?" and the crowd answered, "It's the prophet Jesus from Nazareth in Galilee" (Matt 21:10-11). According to Luke 19, the palm processional is led by Jesus's disciples. A disciple is a personal follower of Jesus. So instead of nameless and faceless crowds, the people who cut down branches and sing Hosanna! are the closest friends of Jesus. When the crowd sang, "*Hosanna* to the Son of David! *Blessings on the one who comes in the name of the Lord! Hosanna* in the highest!" the people were repeating a familiar psalm chanted at major festivals as pilgrims approached the temple[1] (Ps 118:25-26).

These past few years, there has been more information about targeting Asian and Asian Americans and Pacific Islanders (AAPI) with intimidation and violence. Violence toward AAPI women, elders, and LQBTQI+ persons has been happening for hundreds of years. What we are witnessing is new for some, but not new for generations of AAPI.

Far too often, AAPI are shoved to the shadows of society, overlooked in conversations, and simply forgotten. When we dilute some people of color to being white adjacent, we perpetuate a system of intolerance. White adjacent assumes that a person(s) is given more privileges than people of darker skin tone based off of the proximity of their skin tone to white people.

There is a pervasive belief that Asian Americans are the model minority, demonstrated with statements like, "*Those* minorities are hardworking, financially successful people." There is no shortage of shows online that perpetuate the model minority myth. The model minority myth belittles nearly two-thirds of the world's population. According to a Pew Research study, 78 percent of AAPI are born outside of the US.[2] This staggering statistic according to the one study from Harvard Law leads to the greatest gap between the haves and have nots of white, Black, or Hispanic persons.[3] Overlooking the struggle of millions of AAPI discounts their story. The model minority myth is like a free pass to treat AAPI as less than human, without the same agency and dignity other people are naturally afforded. Enshrining the model minority myth continues generations of AAPI women being subject to sexual and physical violence.

What happens when Christians today distill Jesus into a model minority? Jesus, a brown-skinned Middle Eastern man, who is often portrayed with blue eyes and white skin. White Jesus seems more palatable and acceptable. Generations of preachers, teachers, and parents have taught white Jesus. What does your portrayal of Jesus teach the community? Churches across America have countless portraits of serene, white Jesus. When Jesus fits the mold of the model minority, he begins to look like the messiah we want him to be.

This Sunday, for the Christian church, we begin a sacred week called Holy Week. We kick it off by waving our palm branches to welcome Jesus. When Jesus rode a donkey into Jerusalem, the same people singing "*Hosanna* in the highest!" screamed "Crucify him!" just days later. The people who waved palm branches wanted a model messiah who would overthrow the empire; a messiah who would lead the Hebrew people on their terms, under their thumb. After all, that's a big part of the model minority myth. You are safe, when you follow my rules. Seen, but not heard.

Bringing the Text to Life

Do our churches teach about white Jesus as a model minority? Do we preach love with no accountability? Grace with no cost? Gratitude with no grit? Do we weaponize Jesus, the model minority, against the Holy Spirit's movement? Do we preach patience generation after generation? Do we tell people to survive within the institution's rules and turn the other cheek while forgetting all the times Jesus broke religious law? If our religious institutions preach Jesus as a model minority, we run into the danger of diluting the depth of Jesus the Christ.

How are we all complicit in waving our palm branches? When do we shout, "Crucify him!"? We look the other way at injustice. We shout, "Crucify him!" when the organization of religion becomes more important than the Messiah. We shout "Crucify him!" when we rationalize hate crimes. We shout, "Crucify him!" when we blame prostitutes and not the johns. We shout, "Crucify him!" in our silence. There is hope when we remember that Jesus was never white. Let's remember that Jesus marched with the poor and the outcasts. He treated prostitutes and thieves like family. He started a riot while wielding a whip in the temple as he flipped tables over. Jesus held signs like "Black Lives Matter" when he rode into town on a donkey. If a leader rolled into town on a horse, it was a sign that war was coming. Riding a donkey symbolized a time of peace. The power of this symbolism was as clear as holding a "#StopAsianHate" sign. Maybe Jesus has more in common with people of color than we thought. Tame Jesus, Jesus the model minority, is like the person who preaches and teaches Jesus the Messiah, who never said "I don't see color when I see you." Rather, Jesus said he saw our hearts and loved us anyway.

April 6, 2023–Maundy Thursday

Exodus 12:1-4, (5-10), 11-14; *Psalm 116:1-2, 12-19;*
1 Corinthians 11:23-26; John 13:1-17, 31b-35

Riley Short

Preacher to Preacher Prayer

O Lord, as I prepare for Maundy Thursday services, wash me and deliver me from myself that you may be made known. I am not worthy to gather up the crumbs beneath thy table, but show your love, mercy, and grace to me and through me. In the name of Jesus Christ, I claim this gift. Amen.

Commentary

Do you ever buy something that requires putting it together? It might be a piece of furniture, a toy, or something for around the house. I get so excited and want to finish the project that I do not pay attention to the directions. I just want to get it done. Inevitably, I will mess it up and end up following the directions. "When all else fails, follow the instructions."

Our scripture lesson is a list of directions given by God to his people. They are directions on how to celebrate the Passover. We live on this side of the cross and we do well to recall how Jesus followed these directions when he ate the Passover meal with his disciples in the Upper Room on that night before he was crucified.

One of the directives given by God was "This day will be a day of remembering for you" (Exod 12:14). The Lord is instructing us to not forget, to pay attention, and to keep this celebration in our minds. What is it we are to remember? We do well to remember his deliverance.

In the Seder, at the end of the celebration, there is a song traditionally sung in Hebrew that translates "Next year in Jerusalem." It is a song of hope for the captive. The song was sung by the Jewish people who had been taken away from the temple, Jerusalem, and the promised land. It speaks of a hope for deliverance. In the Seder, the people were instructed to remember their deliverance from the bondage of slavery in Egypt and their entrance into the promised land.

We do well to remember the deliverance we have and the hope of deliverance given us. We do well to remember how Jesus added instruction to how we are to celebrate the Passover meal. Let us look at his actions in the Upper Room. He first washed the feet of the disciples. By his example, he instructs us to be a servant.

Preachers would do well to teach again to their congregations about how our stoles are a reminder of how Jesus girded himself with a towel and washed the feet of his followers. Preachers are really educated "foot-washers." All of us are chosen to be servants.

We do well to remember the meaning of the cup and the bread. In the Upper Room, Jesus establishes himself as the Paschal Lamb. The bread is the body of Jesus, the Paschal Lamb. The cup is the blood of Jesus, the Paschal Lamb. And what did he say when he presented the cup and bread that first time in the Upper Room? "Remember Me." It is very much like what the Lord instructed to the Jewish people of old, "This shall be a day of remembering." We remember Jesus, the Paschal Lamb.

We do well to remember the victory given us by Jesus. The Jewish people celebrate their deliverance from bondage and remember it as the greatest act of God in their history. We remember the cross as God's greatest gift. He gave himself as the Paschal Lamb that we may be delivered from slavery to ourselves, our sins, and our foolishness. He gives us deliverance from where we are to where we ought to be.

As we take this cup and take this bread, let us make this a day of remembering. Take it for your comfort, take it—it is a gift to you from a loving God. These are good words of instruction—"Eat this in remembrance of Me."

Bringing the Text to Life

Maundy Thursday is one of those times when the focus should be on the sacrament of Holy Communion and not so much on the preached word. Keep your sermon simple and brief and lift up words we often neglect to heed. The meal and the history of the moment speak for themselves.

The text that excites me the most is from Exodus where we are commanded to celebrate a "Day of Remembering" (Exod 12:14). The preacher can play off the idea of memory, or even the thought of "forgetting" rather than remembering.

What do we remember when we come to the Passover meal on Maundy Thursday? I remember Jesus establishing a new Passover meal. Jesus is the blood of the Passover meal. He is the Paschal Lamb. I remember my ability to betray him, my ability to deny him, my ability to fail, my ability to desert him. But I also remember his great willingness to forgive me and lift me up from my failure to a new path in life. I remember his willingness to show me the way home when I am lost. I remember his willingness to heal me of all my diseases and deliver me from where I am to where I ought to be. I remember that he offers us the cup of grace and the bread of life, reminding all of us that forgiveness and eternal life are freely offered. What a deal! How can I refuse it?

April 7, 2023–Good Friday

Isaiah 52:13-53:12; Psalm 22; Hebrews 10:16-25 or
Hebrews 4:14-16; 5:7-9; John 18:11-19:42

Riley Short

Preacher to Preacher Prayer

O Lord, take me to the foot of the cross that I may be blessed by the full gift of love and grace that pours forth from the given life of Jesus. So, fill me with the truth of the cross that I will be able to share effectively the truth of Good Friday. Amen.

Commentary

There is a lovely story about a young boy who had the annoying habit of speaking in rhyme. One day his preacher father grew exasperated and said, "Son, I am going to spank the poetry out of you." The lad responded, "Oh father, do some pity take and no more poetry shall I make." Thank goodness the father couldn't spank the poetry out of the boy. The boy was Isaac Watts, the writer of some of the great hymns of the church.

One of Watts's hymns is well used on Good Friday, "When I Survey the Wondrous Cross." The third verse of the hymn takes us to the foot of the cross,

See, from his head, his hands, his feet,
sorrow and love flow mingled down.
Did e'er such love and sorrow meet,
or thorns compose so rich a crown?[4]

Watts looks at Good Friday from this side of the cross, but Isaiah sees the event of the cross way before it happened. He describes the act of Jesus on the cross: "He was pierced because of our rebellions and crushed because of our crimes. He bore the punishment that made us whole; by his wounds we are healed" (Isa 53:5).

The prophet in prophetic fashion takes us to the "Good Friday Event." Amazingly, he tells us that "he was oppressed and tormented, but didn't open his mouth. Like a lamb being brought to slaughter . . . he did not open his mouth" (Isa 53:7). Isaiah tells us why this is "Good Friday" instead of "Bad Friday." He explains, "His life is offered as restitution . . . through his knowledge, the righteous one, my servant, will make many righteous, and will bear their guilt" (Isa 53:10-11).

We remember Jesus's words from the cross, "It is finished." He did not say, "I am finished," but "It is finished." What he had finished was the gift of the cross. It is an expression of a feeling that arises when we have finished a task. The act of salvation was complete. It is a "wrap," it is done, it is completed. And here it is all neatly wrapped as a gift for me and for you. The gift has my name on it and your name. It is a gift offered for the taking. But notice it also has the price tag still attached, and the price tag is what we remember whenever we take the elements of Communion. The price is his body and his blood. So, we can take the gift to our comfort. No wonder we call it "Good Friday."

Bringing the Text to Life

The preacher sets the mood for "Good Friday." If it is to be a mournful, sad, and doleful service, the preacher will make it so. There are times when we should be filled with repentance and shame of our failures, but Good Friday is a great time to feature Jesus and his love gift that is so much greater than our foolishness. So, celebrate the action of Jesus, his full gift of love, his mercy and grace, and lift up the saving action of Christ, our Lord.

What greater time than Good Friday to celebrate the Eucharist? The Passover Lamb has been offered. We are no longer under the curse of sin, but are lifted to new life and deliverance from ourselves.

I have always had a special love for the crucifix. When I was a child, we had a neighbor who was a very committed Roman Catholic. She explained the given body of Jesus to me and I have never forgotten. She simply said, "He died for you, my little boy. He died for you." My seminary professor who taught a course titled "Doctrine of Redemption" never could say it so clearly as what she said: "He died for you."

There is a world of people who want to hear that message, who need that message. There are hurting, confused, and lost people who want to experience the love of Christ shown so dramatically on the cross. There is a strange and wondrous drawing power in the cross.

Every day at the end of the day when God was creating the world he said, "It is good." When Jesus was on the cross, he said, "It is finished." Our salvation is complete. It is finished. We can add, "It is good," and that is why we call this day "Good Friday." We have reason to celebrate. We have won through Jesus. How good is that?

April 9, 2023–Resurrection of the Lord/Easter Day

*Acts 16:34-43 or Jeremiah 31:1-6; Psalm 118:1-2, 14-24; Colossians 3:1-4 or Acts 10:34-43; **John 20:1-18** or Matthew 28:1-10*

Riley Short

Preacher to Preacher Prayer

O Lord, take me to the garden where I may discover the empty tomb and sense your living and loving presence. Then may I be filled with the confidence to proclaim the truth of your resurrection. Amen.

Commentary

It is not uncommon in the sporting world to hear of "The Great Comeback." Think of how the New England Patriots came back in Super Bowl LI to beat Atlanta after the Falcons had built up a huge lead. But we gather on Easter Sunday morning to remember the greatest comeback in human history. Jesus who was crucified, dead, and buried has come alive and the word from the tomb in Joseph's garden is "He is not here, He is risen." The comeback of Jesus Christ is the assurance of victory over death, the grave, and sin.

The scripture tells us Mary Magdalene came to the garden tomb while it was still dark. The wise preacher is going to think how members of the congregation know what it is to be where it is "still dark." And yet it is in the darkness that the resurrection glory is discovered. It is strange how often Jesus comes to us in the darkest of times.

Certainly, the world waits in the darkness to hear the latest news from the tomb. And Mary Magdalene is the reporter who covers the story of the great comeback. She reports, she does not edit or add personal opinion—she tells what she has seen, heard, and experienced. She saw the rolled-away stone. The tomb had been sealed, guarded, and was so forbidding. The tormentors of Jesus put the stone there. They brushed their hands and said, "It's over and done with." But Mary finds it rolled away.

In all of our lives there are those stones that seem to defeat us, but the Resurrection reminds us that God has a way of turning them into stepping stones. The latest news from the garden tells us the stone is rolled away.

Mary then sees the grave cloths. When Jesus was born, he was wrapped in "swaddling clothes." In death he is wrapped in "grave cloths." Mary finds they are tossed aside and everyone knows a living body does not need grave cloths. The latest news from the garden is that the grave cloths are no longer needed and they are only slightly used.

Mary reports she has seen an angel. At least she thought at first it was an angel. But she discovers it is Jesus in his risen state. She would have missed such a discovery, but when he called her by her name she knew who it was.

Do you know Jesus loves you and because he loves you he knows your name? What a tender and holy moment when you hear the Lord's still, small voice call you by your name.

The latest news from the garden tomb is that Jesus knows your name.

We need to go to the garden tomb ourselves. We need some stones rolled away. We need to catch a glimpse of the grave cloths. We need to hear Jesus say our name and then return to the darkened world with the good news, "He is risen."

No wonder the great choirs sing in unison today, "Christ the Lord is risen today." And because he lives, so we shall live, forever and ever and ever. Wow, what a comeback!

Bringing the Text to Life

I have always felt Easter was the easiest Sunday for preaching. There is a great sense of celebration evident by the largest crowd of the year. There is great music to support the worship service. There is a feeling of victory over defeat. And I have realized if the stone could not hold back Jesus than neither can I. So, let us be aware that since our victory in Christ is greater than our attempt at preaching, all we need to do is to point at the empty tomb—it speaks loud and clear for itself.

Psalm 118 is a praise hymn that speaks of the attributes of our Lord. The psalm reminds us that God is good and has a faithful love that lasts forever. He is our protection and saving help. He delivers and is victorious. These descriptions of our God are good launching pads for the pastoral prayer.

I am convinced the preacher is wise to stay with the powerful passages from the Gospels. They are familiar and they are the "old, old story." There are times when the familiar is best used and Easter is one of those times. It is hard to improve on the Gospel account of Resurrection Sunday.

John's account of the Resurrection takes us to "the first day of the week" and reminds us that it was "still dark" (John 20:1). The preacher will notice those words, "still dark," and know there are people gathered for worship who know what it is like to be in the dark, outside of a tomb. And Mary Magdalene came to that darkness only to discover the rolled-away stone. Peter and John came running to the tomb and going in saw the tossed-aside grave cloths—they "saw and believed" (John 20:8).

The preacher should well notice that Mary saw not only the empty tomb and the tossed-aside grave cloths, but she saw the living Jesus. She heard him speak to her and, in fact, heard him say her name. After this experience she did not keep it a secret, but she declared, "I have seen the Lord." She could have added, "I have heard him speak my name."

The suggestion for a sermon is simply that the world is waiting in the darkness to hear the latest news from the tomb. It wants to know what we have seen and what we have heard from the Living Christ. Vulnerable people need to hear again, "He is not here; for he has been raised" and "Because he lives we shall also live" (John 28:6; see John 14:19). Wow!

Look for These New Titles from Abingdon Press

The Abingdon Worship Annual 2023
9781791023812
The go-to worship planning resource for all who plan weekly worship. Based on the Revised Common Lectionary.

The Concise Guide for Congregational Care
9781791024109
An essential take-along resource for pastors, care ministers, chaplains, and anyone else who provides spiritual care for people in hospital, hospice, or home settings.

Will You Pray with Me
9781791013431
Teaches methods and techniques for writing and leading prayers in any setting and for any occasion.

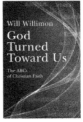

God Turned Toward Us
9781791018894
Learning to "talk Christian"? These reflections on the words the church uses to communicate the faith will bring you closer to God.

The God of the Dangerous Sermon
9781791020224
Is the god behind your preaching a *tribal god* or the *universal God?* Learn to identify and understand which you are serving so you can preach the sermons your community really needs.

Deep Calls to Deep
9781501858956
This deep study of the Psalms demonstrates a new and generative way of reading the Bible—especially relevant during a time of disruption and division.

ORDER THESE AND OTHER RESOURCES AT COKESBURY.COM OR CALL 800-672-1789

Resources published by

⟨⟩|Abingdon Press

April 16, 2023–Second Sunday of Easter

*Acts 2:14a, 22-32; Psalm 16; **1 Peter 1:3-9**; John 20:19-31*

Lynn Bartlow

Preacher to Preacher Prayer

God of life and new life, we celebrate the risen Christ again this day. Help us to experience anew the excitement of the gospel. Give strength to your weary servant, that we might hear and proclaim the good news boldly to the faithful gathered in worship. Amen.

Commentary

On this Sunday after Easter, we are faced with the same story of Doubting Thomas again. We are faced with lower attendance in worship. We are faced with vacationing senior pastors or pastors who are exhausted from the extra that we do for Holy Week and Easter Sunday. Our task for this day remains to make the excitement and joy of Easter continue to resonate and be relevant, even in our weariness, even if we are the guest or occasional preacher. The passage from 1 Peter helps to retain that tone of joy that Easter brings.

First Peter is traditionally believed to be addressed to churches in Asia Minor whose attendees were converts to Christianity from a pagan faith. This letter offers encouragement and instructions to help them live a Christian life in a hostile world. On this week when the crowds are gone from the pageantry of Easter Sunday, those who are left can use a word of encouragement for their own Christian life. The author helps to do that in the very tone that is set from the beginning. Read it again with the excitement of all the exclamation points! "May the God and Father of our Lord Jesus Christ be blessed!" (1 Pet 1:3). Add more exclamation points if you need to! This is good news!!

From there, the author continues to offer good news, from the Resurrection to the inheritance we receive to the faithfulness of God for God's people. Indeed, this is good news that invites us to get the brass and the banners from last week back out for worship. First, we are promised a new birth. But this isn't just any birth; this is birth into a living hope. Because of the good news we celebrated last week, the good news of the resurrection of Christ from the dead, we have a living hope.

This new birth can literally mean a new life on earth. The early church reading this for the first time was leaving behind the pagan lifestyle they knew and was learning what it means to live as Christians. They were leaving behind their relationships to embrace the risen Christ and begin anew. This wasn't easy, but the text offers them encouragement.

Part of the text's encouragement is what awaits us after death. The ultimate prize that awaits us in heaven is that promise of salvation. More than the new life on earth, we have the promise of an inheritance that will never tarnish. It's the promise of God's faithfulness. This is good news!

The promise of Easter is not that we will be insulated from trials. We will all face times of challenges and hostility. It could be open hostility—from coworkers or family who ridicule our choices for a holy life—or it could be trials related to health or employment. No matter what, these trials will lead us to a stronger faith. As we endure through the hard times, we will discover the joy that rests in Christ. In fact, the author invites rejoicing in the face of these hard times. Find joy even in difficult circumstances.

This passage ends with a hint of the gospel lesson for today: "Happy are those who don't see and yet believe" (John 20:29). Although we may not experience the open tomb and the nail-scarred hands for ourselves, we can believe in the new life and living hope that comes from the Resurrection. We can receive that inheritance despite not seeing.

We live in a very visual culture. From movies to YouTube clips to memes on social media, we are inundated with visual images all around us. It is very easy to believe that we must see something in order to truly experience it. It's easy to be like the crowd gathered or like Thomas who desired to see so that he might believe. Jesus, and the author of 1 Peter, reminds us that seeing isn't necessary for believing. Faith allows us to hold on to the promises that we have in Christ Jesus. Happy are those who believe, even if we didn't experience it in the flesh.

Today continues our celebration and joy of Easter. This good news lasts beyond the pageantry and the crowds, into a daily life that offers us joy and promise for each day.

Bringing the Text to Life

First Peter begins with praise. Worship should begin with praise. Our very lives should be couched in praise. How can we praise God more in our lives and in our churches?

You have an opportunity to reflect on inheritances, as the passage names. Our gospel lesson shares the inheritance straight from Jesus, as he gives the gathered disciples peace and joy.

Where have you seen inheritances in your community? Some families deal with inheritances well; others practically split over the dividing of property after a death. Reflect on strange inheritances. My family has passed down a brown bear we named

Rufus that great-great-grandpa hunted; this inheritance now hangs on my teenage son's wall. Or, reflect on inheritances left to your church: did a gift some years ago help your church build a building? Start a ministry? Put you through seminary? Or, explore generational wealth. What's the inheritance the slave owner passes down, compared with the inheritance the slave leaves behind? How does that impact the family, generations later?

April 23, 2023–Third Sunday of Easter

Acts 2:14a, 36-41; Psalm 116:1-4, 12-19; 1 Peter 1:17-23; Luke 24:13-35

Lynn Bartlow

Preacher to Preacher Prayer

Holy One, we come to you today expressing our love for you. We offer our thanksgiving and praise for all that you have done for us, and for the world we minister to. Strengthen us, your servants, to keep our promises to you in these holy times we face. We call on you now to speak to and through us. Amen.

Commentary

The setting of today's text is the Day of Pentecost. The Holy Spirit had come with wind and fire, leaving the disciples able to speak in the tongues of the foreigners who had gathered in Jerusalem. Now the crowd wonders what the commotion is all about. Peter steps up as leader of the group, a position he keeps through Acts 8 to when the focus shifts to Paul.

Peter stands to answer them. We skip most of his sermon, but we get the last of his argument: "Therefore, let all Israel know beyond question that God has made this Jesus, whom you crucified, both Lord and Christ" (Acts 2:36). This assertion is pivotal to what the Christian faith is all about. Peter tells the Jewish crowd gathered for a Jewish festival that they were responsible for the death of Christ. Be careful, preacher. It is easy for us to move to anti-Semitism. Peter makes the case multiple times that he is a Jew, so he is making a critique of the events as one from within. We should be careful in our time that we don't place blame on an entire community of faithful followers.

As a result of Peter's sermon, lives were changed. The Holy Spirit was within Peter and granted the powerful fruit of thousands who were saved. The people heard Peter and accepted his argument. They asked the pivotal question for our text today: "Brothers, what should we do?"

The gospel is not simply a nice story to read to our children. It requires action. When we hear and understand the story of Jesus the Christ, the salvation of God through Jesus Christ, it requires us to do something in return. Even the disciples who were with Jesus on the road to Emmaus realized they had encountered Jesus and they did something: they returned to Jerusalem. Faith demands action. Do we ask anything of our congregation?

Peter tells the crowd that they must do two things: repent and be baptized.

Repentance is a turning away from sin. It's changing the mind and turning back to God. Repentance is key to beginning a life with Jesus. The question is *what* do we need to repent from? The original crowd was told to repent from crucifying Jesus. While they might not have been there when Herod asked them to choose between Barabbas and Jesus, they were guilty by association. This act is what needed repentance at that time.

Note Peter doesn't tell them to repent of a laundry list of ethical problems. That's not what needed repentance at that time. Today, you and I don't need to repent of the act of crucifying Jesus. That was done years ago. Our repentance is from something else, but it's the same call.

This repentance was a call to order our lives in Jesus, who was Lord and Messiah. These titles go back to earlier in Peter's sermon, and serve as reminders that this wasn't just some man, but one who deserves to be noticed. The people were called to reorient their lives by focusing on Jesus, allowing the Spirit to make things new. Today, we are called to do the same.

Following repentance, the crowd is invited to baptism. This is the outward, visible action that validates the inner decision to follow Jesus as Lord and Christ. Baptism was not put off until they reached a certain age or had proven themselves worthy through a class or a test. It was something that tied the believer to the Christian community. In reality, it was a radical break from the norms of society and an alignment with the church. It was a rebirth in real ways for a people who were leaving behind a community of faith and following the risen Christ.

As a result of this repentance and baptism, Peter promises forgiveness of sins and the gift of the Holy Spirit. Forgiveness of sins is a common theme in Luke and Acts. The promise of the Holy Spirit is that promise of Pentecost to all people.

The entire story of Pentecost was an invitation for all people to hear and respond to God through the life, death, and resurrection of Jesus. Peter serves as a powerful witness to what can happen when God's people are convicted by the work of the Holy Spirit.

Bringing the Text to Life

Here, on the Day of Pentecost, Peter sets out the expectation that faith is both personal and communal. Repentance is a personal change. We are certainly called to change the world, but repentance must begin with a personal decision. It's a personal conviction of our need for repentance.

Baptism, then, is the entrance into the community. We are baptized into a community of believers. We are baptized into something greater than ourselves. We need one another to walk the life of faith together. We need one another to hold us accountable as we change, as we continue the work that repentance calls us to.

The story is widely circulated about the soldier who was baptized but held his sword aloft. He felt the need to repent and to be baptized, but not in the area of his work as a soldier. He wanted to turn his life around, give his life to God, but not his life as a soldier. The same story is told of a man and his checkbook; he gave his life to God, but not his checkbook.

April 30, 2023–Fourth Sunday of Easter

*Acts 2:42-47; Psalm 23; 1 Peter 2:19-25; **John 10:1-10***

Lynn Bartlow

Preacher to Preacher Prayer

Bless us, Good Shepherd. May we hear your voice and only your voice as we prepare to lead your people in worship. Allow us to open the gate for others to know of the abundant life you offer. Amen.

Commentary

Like the Second Sunday of Easter, this Sunday is the same, year after year. It's the Shepherding Sunday, where we modern preachers who likely have never even seen a sheep get to interpret this image to our own flocks. Sadly, what we find is that it's been done so often it's hard to say something new!

The image of the people as sheep and God as shepherd is found throughout the Hebrew writings. Of course, David, the shepherd boy turned king, spoke of sheep and shepherding throughout the psalms. The prophets contain the same imagery, from Isaiah 40 to Jeremiah 23 to Ezekiel 34. God is considered the Good Shepherd, with all other shepherds compared to him and found lacking.

Jesus takes the image of the good shepherd and proclaims that he is that person, in verse 14 of this chapter. He is the good shepherd, as God describes it. But that's not really what's here in this passage. In our gospel text for today, Jesus declares that he is the gate for the sheep. A gate is different than a shepherd.

In his commentary on the book of John, William Barclay paints a vivid picture of the two kinds of sheepfolds in the time of Jesus.[5] He describes a sheepfold made of stone that has no gate. Instead, the shepherd lays down as the gate, protecting the sheep for the night. This is a powerful image of a gate, and helps to bring home the point Jesus makes in this passage: Jesus is the one who lays down as a gate, the one who lays down his very life for those who follow him.

As Jesus tells this tale, he speaks of the voice of the shepherd. The sheep know the shepherd's voice, and respond only to that voice. Here, Jesus is calling to mind all the times the voice of God is mentioned in the Bible. The voice is a powerful tool! God speaks, and creation is formed. God calls out to Adam and Eve and they respond by hiding. Moses hears God's voice in the tent of meeting (Num 7:89). God speaks and prophets tremble. In the book of Revelation, God dines with those who hear God's voice and open the door (Rev 3:20). God's voice is powerful and makes things happen.

Jesus claims in this passage that his voice is known by those who follow him. Like sheep who know the shepherd's voice, the followers of Jesus can distinguish the voice of Jesus from those around them. In fact, this is put to the test in the next chapter when Jesus uses his voice to raise Lazarus (John 11:43).

In our day we have many voices calling for our attention. Voices of anger and bitterness. Voices of selfishness and greed. From politicians to media to our own families, we are faced daily with voices from all sides, calling us to spend our time and money and energy on something. Can we hear the voice of Jesus among it all? We know that Jesus is the voice of peace, of love, of grace. The voice of Jesus proclaims a place for all, a banquet awaiting us. The voice of Jesus is the voice inviting in the lost and the forgotten, the poor and the needy.

Our text for the morning is rich with images and reminders that Jesus who was crucified and resurrected brings life—life to the fullest. This life can be found in following the voice of the one who lays down his life for us as the gate.

Bringing the Text to Life

If you haven't heard it, I encourage you to find Bobby McFarrin's version of the Twenty-Third Psalm. Written for his mother, it's a moving rendition of the psalm that's beautifully arranged and shared. It's available multiple places online. If nothing else, let the words and music wash over you as you prepare for worship.

When I was growing up in northern Florida, my family had cows. During the winter, we fed them hay to supplement whatever grass they might be able to find. My dad used the tractor to move a huge, round bale of hay into the pasture. My job was to open the gate, keeping the cows from coming out, and then closing the gate behind the tractor. I would stand around and then open and close the gate again so the tractor could come out and the cows would stay in.

Consider when you have experienced gates. Perhaps you think of a garden gate, meant to keep out deer from the garden. Maybe reflect on a gate in your back yard that keeps your dog in or the neighbor's dogs out. You could also think of a baby gate that keeps your toddler from climbing up or falling down the stairs. Gates are familiar for many of us.

You also might want to consider what it means for someone to know your voice. After we moved to a new house, our kitten began to cry pitifully at night, wandering around downstairs meowing. My husband would call out to him, and the kitten would run upstairs and settle in on our bed. He followed the sound of my husband's voice. He knew his person, and only his person could soothe him.

May 7, 2023–Fifth Sunday of Easter

*Acts 7:55-60; Psalm 31:1-5, 15-16; **1 Peter 2:2-10**; John 14:1-14*

Ron Bartlow

Preacher to Preacher Prayer

God, Author of Salvation, your word is not a static thing held in scrolls or books, but a dynamic, living spirit being written in our hearts and lives. Inspire us not just to recall your wondrous past acts, but to see, to know, and to celebrate your ongoing work within our community today. Amen.

Commentary

How often do I miss the forest for focusing on a single tree, or in the case of these readings miss the "spiritual temple" for focus on one prepared "place" (or "room")? Sometimes my hope and longing for what Jesus is preparing for me after this life keep me from seeing the fullness of community God invites me to partake in now. I jump ahead to Jesus's promise of what he prepares for me, and miss seeing how in the meantime God is connecting me with others to be a part of something miraculous. First Peter 2 invites me to contemplate my place in God's current activity: God's building of Christ-centered community. In a letter that has just described our new birth amid a transitory, fading world (1:23-24), we are all exhorted to cast off that which harms community (2:1) and be built together into something new.

"You yourselves are being built. . . . You are being made. . . ." While we may be the recipients of such activity, the primary actor in this passage is God. God is the builder and maker! We hear of what God is doing with us: building us into a community, founded on the cornerstone of Jesus Christ. The activity is God's, and even the promise made early on—"you will grow into salvation"—is rooted in divine movement: it is God who inspires and provides the "pure," or spiritual, "milk of the word" (vv. 2, 5). God nurtures us and builds us together into something magnificent. What a gift!

Even so, we are not to be idle in the midst of this transformation, as we are linked together into a spiritual temple. We are not dead lumber, but living stones! God's activity is thus bookended with a description of our own. We are initially encouraged to "desire the pure milk of the word," to seek and grow in knowing the accounts of God's salvific activity in our scriptural traditions. At the end we are challenged to "speak of the wonderful acts" of God; to tell our community's story as those who might once have been alone, but have now been invited and included as "God's people" (vv. 2, 9, 10).

The more I meet people in the church communities I serve, the more I realize what they can do that I cannot. I've met engineers who worked on Apollo spacecraft, mechanics who could rebuild my manual transmission, test pilots who broke the sound barrier, hospitality workers who provided service all day with a smile, and teachers who wrote a book of music education. I've been inspired by children who committed to acts of service benefiting strangers, youth whose poetic words challenged my assumptions, and adults who shared the wisdom of experiences radically different from my own. Sometimes as I ponder my place under the stars I do wonder, "Who am I?" Who am I to be among such a great communion of saints? What have I to contribute?

This week's word reminds me that I can always tell of the peaceful assurance I know in my heart because of my inclusion in Christ's new community. I feel assured that Christ not only goes ahead and prepares a room for me (John 14) but I am also confident because of the amazing work God has wrought in my life through these connections with others. The spiritual "milk of the word" of God—be it the written word I read, the spoken word I hear in worship, or the incarnate Word I meet in Jesus Christ—has encouraged, challenged, nourished, and transformed me through time. I can tell how God's wondrous word and work sets me free, makes me whole, and brings me together with others in this amazing community. I can tell of my experiences in this community that is the church, and how I have been nurtured to grow in Christ therein. I can bear witness to how I have been changed and blessed to see the same in others. Sure, there is much to look forward to, but look at how much there is all around us today!

Bringing the Text to Life

We have lots of LEGO bricks in our house; on their own they don't amount to much, but put together we have cars, and robots, and more. Or consider any puzzle photo: a piece on its own might have part of the story, but when we put all 50, or 100, or 500 together the image, and the story, is so much grander! Even so, someone has to take the time to put them together. Thanks be to God! While we might be disparate pieces, God assembles us into something remarkable.

You might consider asking, "What is our church's cornerstone?" You can celebrate the physical cornerstone, perhaps, reflecting on the faith of those who laid it in Christ to build the edifice you worship in today. Projecting photos of the building, and the people, through the years can be a blessing to all. Even better, you can then invite your congregation to look at the many ministries that have been formed and nourished by God's word in your place. What is your church known for? Why do people need you? How is your community changed because of your church's love? Together your community can celebrate its communal response and growth to the "pure," spiritual milk that nourishes you to bear witness to Jesus Christ and to do good in the world.

May 14, 2023–Sixth Sunday of Easter

Acts 17:22-31; Psalm 66:8-20; 1 Peter 3:13-22; John 14:15-21

Ron Bartlow

Preacher to Preacher Prayer

Lord, this Easter season is drawing near its end, and while we may already be looking to the awe and wonder of Pentecostal Spirit, help us continue to declare the empty tomb, the resurrected Christ, and the amazing divine love behind it all. Amen.

Commentary

Two decades ago, I was encouraged to consider how popular culture might be a form of language for my generation (Gen X). Like that episode of *Star Trek: The Next Generation* where Captain Picard struggled to interpret the story-based language of an alien because his universal translator was at a loss for doing so,[1] perhaps the seeming failure of the church to reach my peers had something to do with us speaking a different language. More recently, I have come to wonder if this failure isn't greater than just how we speak. Perhaps we have shifted the presentation of our very spiritual yearnings and their fulfillment away from propositional Christian doctrine and back into mythic, heartfelt story. Has popular culture become the resting house for modern spirituality? If there is any merit to such a notion, I take heart from Paul's experience on Mars Hill.

Quite a lot happens in this second half of Acts 17. Paul is on his own, feels "deeply distressed" (v. 16) by the preponderance of idols, engages those God-fearers aligned with his faith, is invited to speak more widely and does so, and finally has some level of success—"some people joined him and came to believe" (v. 34). A cursory review of both halves of this chapter shows how Paul tailored his message to his audiences in Thessalonica, Berea, and Athens; and the reactions to his accounting of good news varied from hostility to hospitality, from reception to ridicule.

In this week's passage, we read specifically how Paul sought to engage those Athenians who were not predisposed to hear his message. He uses their preexisting expressions of faith to tell them the story of Jesus Christ. "I see how extremely religious you are in every way," he begins (v. 22 NRSV), starting from an awareness of and openness to their shared spiritual yearning. Sure, it culminates in the invitation to "repent" and change (v. 30), but even that challenge is firmly rooted in Paul's assurance that we are united both in our search for, and in the source of, our being (vv. 27-28). With the "respectful humility" that Peter encourages (1 Pet 3:16), Paul speaks to those who will listen about the ground of his hope, linking their expressions of spirituality with his understanding of Jesus Christ, an understanding rooted both in ancient, sacred tradition and personal experience.

In every age, every decade, every generation, there are those among us who feel as though their exploration of the divine—their method of seeking out ultimate truth—is antithetical to or chastised by the existing religious authorities. We always have peers who feel their spiritual search somehow exists outside of the norm, beyond the bounds of what they perceive to be "Christianity." Yet as Paul discovered on Mars Hill, perhaps the expressions we create and paths we pursue all speak to the same foundational spiritual yearnings—yearnings that we can hopefully share find their fulfillment in Jesus Christ.

Psalm 66 reads "come close and listen . . . I will tell you what God has done for me" (v. 16). My starting point for all exegesis and preaching is rooted in the belief that I cannot possibly share declarations of absolute, ultimate truth. Like the psalmist, or the family gathered around the Passover Seder remembering the days of the exodus, I start by placing myself within the greater story of God's activity. Formed by and within traditions held sacred by generations, I speak with the greatest integrity when I draw from my experience of who Jesus Christ is and what Jesus has done. At my best there are moments when, like Paul, I successfully connect my story and these traditions of faith to the spiritual yearning and needs of the people standing before me, inviting them to find their own place in God's ongoing acts of salvation.

Bringing the Text to Life

Is there any week in the lectionary better suited to connecting our Christian faith with spiritual themes from music, movies, television, or other expressions of popular culture than this week we join Paul on Mars Hill? Even if he was distressed, Paul took a minute, looking around and recognizing the spiritual desires of the people around him expressed in their idols. Perhaps we can take a minute, and really look deeply at the popular culture that is resonating with the people we serve. What is stirring their imaginations, inspiring their hearts, and occupying their minds? What is bringing people to tears, or cheers, this week? How might these common cultural images point to some deeper spiritual yearning?

In a world changed by previous years' pandemic and isolation, gearing up yet again for the conflicts of political ideologies, and still struggling with denominational change, some cultural expressions are captivating us because they speak of our deep desires and spark some hope of those desires' fulfillment. The culture around us is, indeed, extremely spiritual—if not religious—in every way, because we are inherently spiritual beings. You might consider how this month's (or quarter's) top movies, television shows, and songs illustrate our common yearnings to know we are part of something greater, that we "live, move, and exist" (v. 28) in God, that we can be something more tomorrow than we are today. Be bold, and connect that which might be speaking to people today to those community traditions and personal experiences of Christ that have led you to where you are.

May 21, 2023–Seventh Sunday of Easter

Acts 1:6-14; Psalm 68:1-10, 32-35; 1 Peter 4:12-14; 5:6-11; John 17:1-11

Ron Bartlow

Preacher to Preacher Prayer

O God, you move in the world around us as the wind of creation, filling us with life. Seasons change—weather warms, students graduate, liturgy shifts—and we are animated and carried by your spirit. You encourage us always to bear witness to your presence and grace. Breathe in us this day, that we may bear faithful witness to the ends of the earth. Amen.

Commentary

Ascension presents us with another theophany: presence, and cloud, and wonder, and perhaps even a bit of incredulity. It may read, "Why are you standing here, looking toward heaven?" but I can hear just a hint of "You're still here? Get up! Get going!" Like the disciples' experience of transfiguration, this fleeting moment where the veil between the spiritual and mundane appears torn and divinity bursts forth is not our lasting home. We may be blessed with mountaintop miracles of respite and retreat, but they are occasions for rejuvenation, empowering us to live and serve faithfully day to day.

The disciples' experience of the ascension is one of assurance and promise. In Luke's narrative the disciples appear still unsure of the nature of the kingdom Jesus has been proclaiming. They ask, likely with some degree of hope, if now is the time for political reformation; if the resurrected Christ is going to miraculously restore the kingdom to Israel. Jesus does not demonstrate such power, but instead promises the disciples will receive power from the Holy Spirit and be witnesses to all the world. And then, he leaves! Jesus ascends—a miraculous moment of validation of who he is as the Messiah, and also a moment of anointing for those left behind.

The promise of power to be provided at Pentecost runs counter to their hope for a deus ex machina political restoration. They are told they cannot just sit back as spectators to watch divine power bring the restoration they hope for. Rather, they themselves will be empowered by the Holy Spirit that they might "bear witness" and bring the work begun in Jesus to all people, everywhere! One can imagine, since the "Acts of the Apostles" is the community's continuation of Jesus's activity as told in Luke, that the disciples' anointing to "bear witness" is to continue the work of Jesus as Jesus understood it (e.g., Luke 4:18-19; 10:25-37; and 19:10). It is almost as if Jesus has replied to their question of political reformation by promising the Holy Spirit and sharing a Facebook meme: "be the change you want to see in the world."

Perhaps there is indeed some incredulity and bewilderment on the part of the disciples as they leave that place of divine appearance. What might it mean that Jesus hasn't restored the kingdom, and instead that they are promised power? Such confusion is only natural, but it is to be short-lived. We anticipate that the arrival of the Spirit on Pentecost will empower this same community to do exactly as Jesus foretells, bearing witness in Jerusalem, Judea, and Samaria, and to the ends of the earth.

In the meantime, though, whether they be pondering Jesus's answer to their question or faithfully waiting for the promised power of the Holy Spirit, the community wisely leans on the presence of God, "united in their devotion to prayer" (1:14). This Pentecostal anointing that will lead them as Spirit-filled witnesses to preach to thousands, this receiving and responding to the gift of God's presence that will lead to the church's power to lead life-change, begins with a community united in prayer. Whether we are still contemplating who Jesus is or prayerfully asking for direction to lead change, the Holy Spirit is about to move in us that we might move in the world.

Bringing the Text to Life

Perhaps this is a week for the community to be "united in their devotion to prayer" to mark significant changes and transitions. How is your community praying for graduates and their families? How might you pray for the empowerment of those preparing to enter the workforce for the first time? Is your congregation boldly moving with a ministry plan, or perhaps entering a fallow summer season in which to pray for the empowerment of the Holy Spirit for the year ahead?

The ascension of Christ is very much like a hand-off; the game goes on, but the ball is in our hands. Training prior to and coaching during the game will guide us, but we have to take the ball and run with it. Perhaps you can notice and celebrate areas in your community where such hand-offs are occurring today.

This may be silly, and is my own story, but an experience with a ladder comes to mind. My very first paid job was as an assistant to the janitor in my local church. One day he set up a tall ladder, handed me a couple of those old-style, long, fluorescent bulbs, and asked me to climb up and change them. I got three rungs up before I had to come down; I just couldn't do it. He assured me I was fine, then got the senior pastor, who came out from his office, took the light bulbs, and climbed the ladder. At the time I had no inclination of going into ministry, but that pastor said to me, "If you ever think of ministry, remember this: sometimes you have to do what others aren't ready or able to." Years later, I have done many things I might not have thought myself capable of, because of the wisdom, encouragement, and faith that has been handed off to me by others empowered by the Holy Spirit.

May 28, 2023–Day of Pentecost

Acts 2:1-21; Psalm 104:24-34, 35b; **1 Corinthians 12:3b-13**;
John 20:19-23

Steve Price

Preacher to Preacher Prayer

Gracious God, provider of every gift, I thank you that through the same Spirit that was present on the day of Pentecost, you continue to bless the church today with the gifts we need to fulfill your purposes. Prepare me to use my gift faithfully this week, that in the preaching of your Word we might all hear your calling on our lives once again. Amen.

Commentary

It is Pentecost Sunday, and most church attendees on this day will likely anticipate hearing the Acts 2 story about the birth of the church. Many will come assum-
ing that the sermon will be based on this text. Thanks to the lectionary, however, the
preacher is not without other options for the day. What if this year for Pentecost,
you still incorporate the Acts 2 story into the worship experience (perhaps a video, a
responsive reading, an interpretive dance?) while in the sermon focusing attention on
an alternative text instead.

The reading from 1 Corinthians offers a poignant witness of the Holy Spirit at
work in the church from its beginnings all the way to today. This passage will certainly be another familiar one for many in the congregation, especially anyone who
has ever taken a spiritual gifts assessment. The repetition of two words throughout the
text, different and same, is worth exploring as a way to frame the day's message. We
discover in these verses that, in order for the church to fulfill its mission to the world,
both differentness and sameness are needed. There are differences in the way God has
created and gifted us, yet it is the same Spirit that is present and at work in the lives
of all who are members of the body of Christ.

Interestingly, Paul uses a trinitarian formula in verses 4-6 to further elaborate
on the presence of both differentness and sameness within the body, serving as a

reminder that these qualities also exist within God's own self. It is the same Spirit, he tells us, that is responsible for the distribution of all the different gifts that make up the body; it is the same Lord who is over all the different ministries that emerge from the body; and it is the same God who is responsible for all the different activities performed by the body.

One other thought about how same and different work together for the good of the church and its mission through the gifting of the Spirit: notice that it is in the differentness of gifts within the body that order is established. A word of wisdom is given to one, faith to another, gifts of healing to another. If all had the same gift . . . now that would be chaos. Or, to put it as Paul does a little later in the chapter, "If all were one and the same body part, what would happen to the body?" (v. 19). But thanks be to God that the variety of gifts are distributed in such a way that, when offered under the lordship of Christ, they serve the common good (v. 7).

The presence of this pair of opposites, different and same, in the passage as in the church serves as a reminder to the congregation on this day of Pentecost: the kind of community the Spirit comes to form among us is not based on uniformity. Rather, the gathered body of believers is beautiful in its diversity, held together in our common confession of faith in Christ.

Bringing the Text to Life

Consider sharing examples of other settings where the characteristics of both differentness and sameness are essential to fulfilling a purpose or vision. For example, you might use a sports analogy, where not all the participants on a particular team play the same position or fulfill the same role. A football team would not fare very well, for example, if everyone who came out to play was a wide receiver. The differentness of the members makes it possible for the team to have all the parts it needs to thrive. Yet, equally necessary for performing at maximum potential is a shared focus and a mutual commitment to supporting and building one another up in pursuing the team's goal.

The preacher might then recall a time when the church (whether the local congregation or another community of faith) has thrived thanks to both the qualities of differentness and sameness being present and affirmed. Perhaps you even reflect on a time when the church had to patiently wait for the right people to come along to complete the array of gifts needed, making it possible for the congregation to fulfill the particular purpose or mission to which the Spirit was leading them. Taking time to acknowledge examples from the past of how the Spirit has equipped the church through a diversity of gifts needed can serve as an encouragement for the future.

Today is also a great opportunity to acknowledge those whose gifts are different from the ones we typically associate with roles and opportunities in the life of the church. There are surely people in your congregation who have gifts to share, but who question where (or even if) their particular gift could be used within a church setting. Let this day be a time of inviting them into prayer, conversation, and discovery of how God might be looking precisely for their gift for the building up of the body of Christ.

June 4, 2023–First Sunday after Pentecost

Genesis 1:1–2:4a; Psalm 8; 2 Corinthians 13:11-13; **Matthew 28:16-20**

Steve Price

Preacher to Preacher Prayer

O God, we can never fully comprehend the wonderful mystery of who you are, Great Three-in-One. Nevertheless, we give thanks for grace that opens our eyes and deepens our awareness. This week, as we celebrate your trinitarian presence among us, renew our commitment to bear witness to you and your love in the world. Amen.

Commentary

It is Trinity Sunday, a day that goes unmentioned and unrecognized in many churches each year. Some preachers may find the thought of a sermon on the Trinity too daunting on the one hand or too boring on the other. While the subject is certainly daunting, it is anything but boring. Perhaps a good place to start in our preaching this week is to acknowledge that we can never fully exhaust all there is to say, nor will any of our metaphors, images, or names fully capture who the trinitarian God is.

The Gospel of Matthew offers us the only instance of the traditional trinitarian formula in all of Scripture: "in the name of the Father and of the Son and of the Holy Spirit" (v. 19). What does it mean to baptize in this name? One opportunity available to the preacher this week is to talk about the Trinity as the basis for a very particular type of community—the one that Jesus inaugurates through assigning the Great Commission to his disciples.

Steering the sermon in this direction, the preacher could explore the relationship that exists within God's own self as the model for the type of relationships meant to exist within the church. What we find within the Trinity is perfect harmony and mutuality. The different members of the Trinity are never at cross-purposes with one another. Scriptural examples of the harmonious presence of all three persons of the Trinity include the moment of Jesus's baptism, when the Holy Spirit descends and words of blessing are heard from the Father, "This is my Son, the Beloved, with whom I am well pleased" (3:17 NRSV). Then just last week, we celebrated Pentecost, remembering the day when the specific work of the Spirit was to breathe life into the birth of the church, where people of all languages might find themselves united as children of God through faith in Jesus Christ.

The Trinity as model for Christian community also reveals that love need not be binary or finite, and that in fact God invites us into loving in a way that always makes room for the other. This indeed is an extraordinary kind of love for which God alone can equip us. William Placher captures the idea well: "Nothing is rarer or more magnificent than to wish that another be loved equally by the one whom you love supremely and by whom you are supremely loved."[1]

Reflecting on what we learn about the character of God through the doctrine of the Trinity and what it has to teach us about our own communities might then lead the preacher into observation and examination. Where does our current witness (whether the local congregation or the global church) show evidence that we have embraced the kind of community we see reflected in God's own self? Where must we confess that there is work to do?

Finally, the sermon could lead the congregation to the table, where we experience the wide-open love, present within God's own self, extended outward. An invitation to come and feast as members of a particular community where all are welcome is quite a compelling embodiment of that love. And of course, it is the perfect day to welcome new members into that community through the sacrament of baptism.

Bringing the Text to Life

Colin Gunton wrote, "Overall, there is a suspicion that the Trinity is a bore . . . a matter of mathematical conundrums and illogical attempts to square the circle."[2] Even if they might not articulate it quite this way, many in your congregation may also anticipate a sermon on the Trinity to be boring. Surprise them this week with an approach that transforms the Trinity in their minds from static doctrine to a powerful witness of who God is.

Visuals can be a wonderful teaching tool. The ideas shared here can help you address some of the historic shortcomings of explanations of the Trinity while also enabling your congregation to imagine in new ways the relationships that exist within God's own self. (Note: having these visuals on display near the altar or pulpit can heighten curiosity and anticipation as people are entering for worship.)

For example, three different pieces of fruit (an apple, a pear, and an orange, perhaps) can be used to talk about the matter of substance. While they are all fruits, they are of different substance. The historic affirmation of the church, on the other hand, has been that the three members of the Trinity are of the same substance. Three dining utensils (a fork, a knife, and a spoon) can be used to illustrate the matter of function. People often associate each member of the Trinity with particular and sometimes separate functions, but the witness of scripture and the church is that all members of the Trinity are present in all functions. Three album covers from your favorite band or musical artist can be used to demonstrate temporal relationship, which sometimes gets applied to the Trinity. Unlike the albums, which have a sequential order in the band's history, the doctrine of the Trinity affirms that all three members are all fully present throughout and beyond history.

Having used these illustrations to reveal a frequent shortcoming in our attempts to explain the Trinity (i.e., that the work of the Trinity can be separated or divided by member), the preacher is now ready to share one that better reflects mutuality. Give the congregation a visual experience of perichoresis, or the divine dance, by juggling (or asking a church member who knows how) to show how the three members of the Trinity are constantly "passing into one another."[3]

June 11, 2023–Second Sunday after Pentecost

Genesis 12:1-9; *Psalm 33:1-12; Romans 4:13-25;*
Matthew 9:9-13, 18-26

Steve Price

Preacher to Preacher Prayer

Holy God, when you call us out of our places of comfort and familiarity, help us remember that you never do so without offering a blessing. I give thanks this week for the ways you have blessed me along the way since leaving my nets behind to follow you in this wild adventure of ministry. May the recollections of your faithfulness to me inspire my preaching, so that I might invite others to step out in faith and find joy in your calling on their lives. Amen.

Commentary

Today's lectionary passage from the Hebrew Scriptures inaugurates the story of God choosing a particular people through whom God will bless all people. God selects Abram, the son of Terah, who had settled his family in Haran. The message is direct and (literally) unsettling: "Leave your land, your family, and your father's household" (Gen 12:1).

Abram has no time to recollect himself from this startling announcement before a sequence of action verbs comes flying at him (and us). In rapid succession, we hear the promises attached to God's command: "I will show," "I will make," "I will bless," "I will curse" (vv. 2, 3).

We are not told why the Lord has chosen this particular man and his wife, Sarai, for the assignment, and quite frankly they would already appear to be unlikely candidates. After all, the verses that precede our text for today let us in on the knowledge that Sarai has been unable to have children. Nevertheless, these early verses make clear that God intends to be the initiator in the story that is to unfold through Abram.

What follows is precisely the kind of faith-filled response for which God is looking. Abram packs up everyone and everything of value to him and leaves the familiar for the uncertain, relying on God to keep the promises that have been made. By the time he and his clan pull off the highway at the first rest stop, the oak of Moreh, God has seen enough of Abram's faith to deliver one more promise for today: "I give this land to your descendants" (v. 7). Abram's reaction is to build an altar and worship the Lord, a pattern that he will repeat throughout his God-inspired journey.

This opening episode of the Abrahamic covenant story introduces us to God's commitment to bless Abram and his descendants. It also introduces us to Abram's willingness to trust that commitment. The prototype of faithful obedience is established through Abram, whose example is rehearsed in multiple places in the New Testament, including today's epistle text. His witness of stepping out into the unknown also finds a parallel in today's gospel story of Matthew the tax collector, leaving behind the familiar life that he knew in order to follow Jesus.

It's worth mentioning that the story closes for today on the ominous note that Abram "set out toward the arid southern plain" (v. 9). Who would have imagined that the direction God would lead Abram first in this journey by faith would deposit him in a barren, drought-ridden land? Apparently, God's plans for blessing Abram do not include instant gratification or immediate prosperity. We are left eager to hear more about how the story will unfold, and when the promises of God will begin to be realized by Abram and his family.

Bringing the Text to Life

Most people in your congregation have had a significant experience in their lives of leaving. Some have left a job that they loved or a town where they had deep roots. Others have left a particular house where they lived for years or even decades. Leverage this memory and the emotions attached to it to help them connect with today's story.

Most of the time, in our experiences of leaving we at least had some idea of where we were going next. Without such knowledge, would the decision to leave have been too unsettling for us to follow through? Abram left his home with no idea of where he was headed. He would have to be totally reliant upon God to lead him to "the land that I will show you" (v. 1). Yet, God did not leave Abram empty-handed or completely blind to what was ahead. God made promises to Abram about what God had in mind for him, a future that included land, descendants, and blessing.

The preacher might see today's text as an opportunity for encouraging the congregation to lean into the uncertainty of life with a confidence in God's providence. Is there a leave-taking they recognize that needs to happen in their personal lives in order to live more faithfully, but of which they are afraid? Is there a change within the church that they know is good and necessary for the future, but which they have been resisting out of fear?

Even when the road is unclear, and perhaps even when what seems immediately in front of us is hard and uncomfortable, the faith-filled life looks forward in expectation of the blessing that is coming. You might help the congregation anticipate such an outcome by sharing an example of when it has been true before.

Is there a story of leaving the familiar from your own experience where you did not know what lay ahead, but you stepped out in faith and ultimately sensed God's blessing? Is there a member of the church who could offer testimony from her own life or from the church's story where she has seen this to be true? Witnesses to God's faithfulness in the past can bolster trust in God's steadfast commitment to blessing our futures.

June 18, 2023–Third Sunday after Pentecost

Genesis 18:1-15, (21:1-7); *Psalm 116:1-2, 12-19; Romans 5:1-8; Matthew 9:35-10:8, (9-23)*

Jason Micheli

Preacher to Preacher Prayer

Living and Loquacious Lord, forgive us preachers for so often forgetting in our everyday lives what we delight in proclaiming in the pulpit on Sunday mornings; namely, that you choose the most absurd and unlikeliest of sinners for your good and gracious ends.

Commentary

Did you ever notice how quickly God raised the degree of difficulty in the Bible? "Adam, don't eat the fruit of that tree in the garden. Noah, build me a boat. Abraham, cut off the tip of your. . . ." To which Abraham surely replied, "Um . . . can't I just build you a bigger boat?"

There's not a lot of laughter in the Bible. By my reckoning, there's only two instances of laughter in all of scripture. One place is today's passage in Genesis 18. While her husband entertains God himself unawares, Sarah eavesdrops from the flap of the tent. She hears the promise of a child as a punchline. And why wouldn't she? This was four thousand years before the invention of Viagra. Before we pile on Sarah, I should point out Sarah laughs because she's hearing God's redemptive promise for the first time. Abraham sat on this promise for almost three decades.

It's funny, these are not impressive people. Of all the people in the world, God chose these two for his redemptive purpose. God works his redemptive purpose through ungodly people like them so that good people like us will realize that we do not contribute anything to God's promised work of redemption. The only thing we contribute to our redemption is our resistance.

No sooner has Sarah heard this promise than she's urging Abraham to hurry its happening by sleeping with their servant, Hagar. Like her we hear the promise and then we refuse to believe its happening isn't our responsibility. That's what we're supposed to take away from this question God asks us: "Why are you laughing? Is anything too hard for God?" Notice, God didn't ask, "Is anything too hard for you when you've partnered with God?" When it comes to God's work to redeem the world from the powers of sin and death, you and I bring nothing to the table. Abraham and Sarah have "no ground for boasting." That's how the Apostle Paul speaks of them in Romans. They simply trusted, eventually, that the Living God is able. They simply trusted God's word and, by their faith, the Apostle Paul says, God reckoned it to them "righteousness."

Paul is no one's idea of a comedian, but here's the funny thing and Paul, a Hebrew who wrote in Greek, assumes you're in on the joke. That word *righteouness* in Hebrew and in Greek (in other words, in the entire Bible) is the same word as *justice*. In scripture, *justice* and *righteousness* are nouns that function with the force of a verb. And verbs do work. Therefore, this noun with the force of a verb belongs to God. Absurd and unfaithful people like Abraham and Sarah are the objects of God's verb. The Living God is able to draw you into his right-making work in the world.

Bringing the Text to Life

One of my best friends is a lawyer named Brian Stolarz. He'd be the first to admit he brings nothing to the table. Brian grew up Catholic and works at a fancy white-collar firm. Because he'd come up as a public defender in New York City and because he had a good BS radar, a few years ago Brian's firm asked him to head up a death penalty case in Texas, a case his firm had taken pro bono. It was one of those bleeding-heart cases firms take to boast about themselves to their paying clients and prospective hires.

It was a cop-killing at a check-cashing store in Houston. With no DNA, the DA had prosecuted Dewayne Brown, a mentally handicapped black man with no record whose IQ the state doctors ginned up a few points so the prosecution could notch another win. After Brian visited Dewayne for the first time on death row, he walked out into the parking lot, his heart racing, and he threw up on the pavement. It hadn't really occurred to Brian until after meeting Dewayne that Dewayne was innocent.[4]

Dewayne's free now. And so Brian is free to tell his part of the story: how the case almost ruined his marriage; how it hurt his career; how it made him a stranger to his young kids; how if it was up to him and he could do it all over again, he wouldn't. Brian said to me one night in a Taco Bell drive-thru: "I'm not a social justice warrior. I grew up Catholic hearing that the death penalty was wrong. And then—out of the blue—it was thrust upon me [pay attention to how he puts it]. It was like God put this good work in front of me to do. Still, I didn't want to do it. I felt compelled—something compelled me—to do it in spite of what maybe I wanted to do. It's funny—it's like our definitions of activism aren't passive enough."

June 25, 2023–Fourth Sunday after Pentecost

*Genesis 21:8-21; Psalm 86:1-10, 16-17; **Romans 6:1b-11**; Matthew 10:24-39*

Jason Micheli

Preacher to Preacher Prayer

Lord, forgive us preachers for treating the proclamation of your living Word as but one among the many tasks of ministry. No doubt, Lord, you know better than we do that we do not preach sermons, particularly sermons about the cross and "freedom," that can rival the liturgies of red, white, and blue that form our listeners. It's not yet the Fourth of July, Lord, but the Apostle Paul has a word from you about freedom. Given our track record, Lord, we need your help.

Commentary

In Romans 6, Paul builds on his argument by showing you how Jesus is the Second Moses, how Christ has delivered us from the domain of sin and death so that we might walk in newness of life. And that word walk is key. It's "halakah." It comes from the exodus, when God, through Moses, rescued his people from slavery in Egypt and delivered them to a new life by parting the Red Sea so that they could walk across it on dry land.

Paul's point is that through our baptism we leave the old world and we are liberated into God's new creation; so that, as baptized Christians, we might live lives in the here and now that make intelligible Christ's cruciform Kingdom. That's what Jesus means by "eternal life." For Paul, the Resurrection inaugurates a new reality in the world, so that baptism is for us what the Red Sea was for the Israelites: a doorway into a new Kingdom, a new and different and distinct people in the world. That's what Paul means when he says elsewhere that all the old national and political and ethnic distinctions do not matter because the baptized are now united in Christ. For Paul, baptism isn't so much the outward symbol of a believer's faith. Baptism unites us into Christ so that what is true of him is now true of us, and what's true of him is that he has been raised from the dead and exalted to the right hand of God where he is the Lord over the nations of the Earth.

For Paul, then, baptism is our naturalization ceremony in which allegiance and loyalty is transferred from the kingdoms and nations of this world to the Kingdom of God. In our epistle we're to hear echoes of the Christ hymn in Philippians 2:9-11, "Therefore, God highly honored him and gave him a name above all names, so that at the name of Jesus everyone in heaven, on earth, and under the earth might bow, and every tongue confess that Jesus Christ is Lord, to the glory of God the Father." To confess that Jesus Christ is Lord is to profess that something fundamental has changed in the world, something to which we're invited to believe and around which we're called to reorient our lives and for which, if necessary, we're expected to sacrifice our lives. To confess that Jesus Christ is Lord is to profess that at Easter God permanently replaced the way of Caesar, the way of the world, with the way of Jesus, a way that blesses the poor, that comforts those who mourn—a way where righteousness is to hunger and thirst after justice and where the Kingdom belongs to those who bear crosses, not to those who build them.

Bringing the Text to Life

"Don't change *anything* for the first six months. Earn their trust. Don't do or say anything provocative. Don't ruffle feathers. Don't upset anyone. Don't rock the boat. Be as inoffensive and ordinary as possible. Don't worry, that's not a comment about you. I give the same advice to every new pastor."

That was the advice I received from a seminary professor shortly before I graduated. I soon discovered his advice was incompatible with the fact that United Methodist pastors in Virginia celebrate their first Sunday in their new churches the weekend everyone else in America is celebrating the red, white, and blue. I hadn't yet unloaded the moving truck when my new secretary informed me that I had been scheduled to preach the sermon at the annual, ecumenical Independence Day service. "But Independence Day isn't even a Christian holiday," I said.

When I arrived at the pavilion area, I spotted a large, wooden cross in the center of the stage—the kind of cross you'd see on the side of the highway. Only this cross had a large, car dealership–sized American flag draped over it.

I walked up to a guy who looked like the master of ceremonies, a Pentecostal preacher, it turned out. I introduced myself and then I said: "Say, maybe we should take the flag off the cross before people show up for the service and get upset."

The Pentecostal preacher just stared at me, the same soothsaying way my secretary had, and then he said: "Why would anyone get upset? This is the Independence Day service after all."

I threw my sermon manuscript in the trash, and said to the Holy Spirit, "All right, Lord, you stuck me in this place. It's on you now."

And I spoke to them about the Jesus who not only died for their sins but who was raised to the Father's right hand to be given, right now, dominion over the earth.

"As wonderful as this nation is," I said, "we are not God's Beloved because Jesus Christ is God's Beloved and through the waters of baptism, as the Red Sea before us, we have been made subjects of his reign."

The response to the sermon reminded me that allegiance to this King can be an uncomfortable form of citizenship among the nations.

July 2, 2023–Fifth Sunday after Pentecost

*Genesis 22:1-14; Psalm 13; **Romans 6:12-23**; Matthew 10:40-42*

Jason Micheli

Preacher to Preacher Prayer

Almighty God, equip those, whom, in your folly, you have called to preach, to proclaim your word faithfully, of course, but also simply and clearly, so that those whom you have called as your disciples might learn how to speak Christian.

Commentary

As much as it is anything else, Christianity is a language, and to be a Christian is, in no small measure, to work with words that possess particular meanings—meanings that are determined by the Word who was made flesh. In other words, what we talk about when we talk about the word *freedom* is not necessarily—or rather, is necessarily not—what others talk about when they talk about freedom.

In writing about language and the training that language requires, the philosopher Stanley Cavell recalls a memory from his daughter's childhood.[1] From an illustration in one of her very first board books as a toddler, Cavell's daughter learned to say the word *kitty*. Some weeks later, however, the little girl came across a fur coat—a mink—stroked it, and said the word *kitty*, making Cavell realize that his daughter really did not know what the word *kitty*, means. The word *kitty* had a more specific definition than his daughter yet understood. Only when she gets to pet a litter of kittens, Cavell suggests, will she "walk into speech."

What is the speech into which Paul would have us walk when it comes to the peculiar, counterintuitive way he uses this word *freedom*? When the Apostle Paul announces today that Christ has freed us, the speech Paul would have us walk into—and be schooled by—is the language of the exodus. Seldom do we notice, but when God gives the Law to the Israelites at Mount Sinai he does so in order to set them free from captivity to false gods. The commands of the Law are not the limits God sets around his people's freedom. The commands of the covenant are the way God sets his people free. Free from what? How does God telling us what to do constitute freedom?

The late Catholic theologian Herbert McCabe argues in his book, *Law, Love, Language*, that all ten commandments of the Decalogue—as well as the hundreds of other laws of the Mosaic covenant—are meant to reiterate the first commandment, "I am the Lord your God, who brought you out of the land of Egypt, out of the house of slavery; you shall have no God but Yahweh, the God who sets you free."[2] Thus the Law, McCabe says, is actually a Charter of Liberation. The commandments are ways we learn to live not as slaves to the false gods—and very often we're our own false gods—but as subjects of the true and living Lord.

That God tells us what to do with our bodies, for example, is a reminder that we are not gods; therefore, the bodies of others are not objects to which we're entitled. That God commands us not to kill and to love our neighbor as ourself, even the neighbor who is also our enemy, is a reminder that we are but creatures and that this is the form our Creator's care of us took.

To assert, as Paul has in his Letter to the Galatians, that the purpose of the Law is not to justify you is not to suggest that the Law has no purpose. The purpose of the Law is to teach you how to be a creature. It's not about being justified. It's about becoming fully human.

We live at a time and in a culture that defines freedom the way the Bible defines sin: complete autonomy. But the word *autonomy* in Greek, *auto* + *nomos*, literally means to be a Law unto your own self, which is as good a definition as any for god-lessness. To be free, our culture tells us, is to be free from external constraints and from the claims of others. That Christianity is a foreign language in such a culture can be illustrated by the fact that ancient and medieval Christians depicted hell as the realm where the unrepentant are granted the prerogative to do whatever they want to do. At such a time and in such a culture, therefore, that God has told us what to do, that God has given us something to do is not a burden but a gift.

Bringing the Text to Life

My oldest son left for a semester abroad just as the withdrawal from Afghanistan was happening in August 2021. His flight left early Wednesday just past midnight so we were at Dulles late on a Tuesday night to see him off.

I was expecting to cry. I was not expecting to cry because of the rows upon rows of Red Cross cots I saw set up throughout the terminal and the huddled groups of Afghan refugees holding frightened children and plastic bags of belongings.

After my son checked his luggage, we left the ticketing desk.

Walking with him toward the security checkpoint, I bumped into a young woman exiting a restroom. She was wearing a light-pink hijab and held an impossibly tiny baby across her chest. Both of them, baby and mother, had dirt and blood on their clothes and cheeks.

I bumped into her and, in an instant, a news story, from which I had heretofore been comfortably removed, collided into me.

"I'm sorry, excuse me," I said, hoping to avoid tearing up in front of her.

As I helped her pick up belongings, I thought of the law, "Welcome the refugee among you and care for them, for once you were a refugee in the land of Egypt" (Lev 19:33-34 NIV).

Bumping into her was like walking into speech. To be so reminded of my obligation to someone like her—it wasn't a burden. It was a gift. I left the airport that night more what God made me to be. That's freedom. That's the freedom into which Christ has delivered us through cross and resurrection.

But to so understand freedom is to speak a strange and difficult language in a foreign culture whose words often mean otherwise. Fortunately, Christ has given us the bread and wine that is his body and blood; neighbors and possibly even enemies; the poor, whom we always will have with us—so that, for a world in need of witnesses, we might learn to walk into this speech.

July 9, 2023–Sixth Sunday after Pentecost

*Genesis 24:34-38, 42-49, 58-67; Song of Solomon 2:8-13;
Zechariah 9:9-12; Psalm 45:10-17; **Psalm 145:8-14**;
Romans 7:15-25a; Matthew 11:16-19, 25-30*

Kevin Murriel

Preacher to Preacher Prayer

Lord of restoration and peace, may your presence grant us the ability to praise you in the midst of pain and to seek you in times of trouble. Help us to rejoice in your faithfulness and seek your goodness daily. In Jesus's name. Amen.

Commentary

Psalm 145 is a psalm of praise written by King David in the postexilic period of Israelite history. God's people have returned to Jerusalem after Babylonian exile, rebuilt the temple, and are seeking to reestablish their worship identity and practices. In this psalm, David teaches the people how to rejoice from generation to generation about God who always remains faithful. Psalm 145 reveals David's heart of worship. His desire is to point the people to the worship of the King of kings. The psalm opens with these powerful words: "I will lift you up high, my God, the true king. I will bless your name forever and always" (v. 1).

David's intent is to lift God above even his own kingly position and therefore, direct God's people to acknowledge God as their daily sufficient source. He is proclaiming that God is the infinite source of all there is and will ever be. This takes humility and selflessness. David was a powerful king, and he humbly declares how glorious and wondrous the works of God have been throughout the generations (vv. 5-7)—and he's right. Only God could deliver them out of the cruelty of Babylonian exile. Only God could raise up prophets like Jeremiah and Isaiah (and others) to deliver God's messages to those in captivity. Only God could perform signs and wonders through Hebrew servants like Shadrach, Meshach, Abednego, and Daniel while in exile. And it was only God who could orchestrate a reentry back to Jerusalem using

Ezra, a priest, and Nehemiah, a cupbearer, who would lead the rebuilding of the walls and reestablish order within the city.

David, in verses 8-14, is making the case that God's reign will last forever and therefore we must praise God accordingly. Finally, this psalm is a reminder that God is always merciful and present with us. David says in verse 14, "The Lord supports all who fall down, straightens up all who are bent low." This was both Israel's and David's testimony. Throughout history, the Israelites would serve God and then fall into idol worship, but God never abandoned them. After they endured a period of struggle, the Lord restored them. David, personally, experienced God's mercy through countless missteps and bad decisions during his reign as king. So, the praise that David offers is from a place of gratitude that God didn't end the story of the Israelite people or his personal narrative after a bad chapter. God, the author of life and the giver of mercy, continues to lift those who are bent low, and therefore, God should be praised above all else.

Bringing the Text to Life

Has there ever been a season in your life where you struggled through something and God held you up? Perhaps you can ask your listeners to think about a time when they got things wrong or made a mistake, and the mercy of God gave them another chance. When my daughter started riding her bike for the first time, she took her foot off the pedals and became unstable, almost falling off the bike. She didn't get hurt because I was there, only a few feet behind her, ready to catch her if she started falling. She was startled and was nervous to continue riding, but her assurance was that her father was there to pick her back up and help her to keep going.

Use a story similar from your personal experience and tie it into how God is always there to pick us up and to direct us when we stumble or fall. You could also talk about the importance of praising God above all else. We should put more energy into praising God than we do our material possessions, people, or those habits that we make our idols.

If you use props in your sermon, this would be a great opportunity to show examples of idols (i.e., work, consumerism, people, etc.) and make God visually larger than those. You could attach strings to the idols and then attach each string to yourself to show how many directions things other than God can pull you in. You could also use this illustration to frame the historical context of the Israelites' relationship with God and how they worshipped idols that led them away from God.

When you read the words of David throughout Psalm 145, he is giving unashamed praise to God. It's exuberant. You could construct a sermon that helps your hearers understand why God is worthy of such exuberant praise. This is a psalm of celebration summoning listeners to a time of reflection and jubilation that God desires to turn their sorrow into joy!

July 16, 2023–Seventh Sunday after Pentecost

Genesis 25:19-34; Isaiah 55:10-13; Psalm 65:(1-8), 9-13;
*Psalm 119:105-112; **Romans 8:1-11**; Matthew 13:1-9, 18-23*

Kevin Murriel

Preacher to Preacher Prayer

Gracious God, help us to live in the assurance of the resurrection of Christ Jesus, who freed us from condemnation through His power and grace. May we live with the freedom and faith to overcome sin and delight in your goodness all of our days. In Jesus's name. Amen.

Commentary

The Apostle Paul begins Romans 8 with some very good news: "There is therefore now no condemnation for those who are in Christ Jesus" (8:1 ESV). This statement highlights the reality that many feel condemned, by people and God, but through Christ, we have freedom from condemnation. Paul's statement raises the question, "why would one feel condemned?" How might listeners to the preaching of this text connect with times in their lives where they felt condemned by God or even unworthy of the love of God?

In verses 2-8, Paul makes distinctions between the flesh and the spirit and concludes with a bold statement in verse 8 (ESV), saying, "Those who are in the flesh cannot please God." By "in the flesh," Paul is referring to those who are not led by or open to the guidance of the Holy Spirit. He references their mindset in 8:5a ESV when he says, "For those who live according to the flesh set their minds on the things of the flesh." The goal, then, for Paul's message in Romans 8 is to encourage all people to seek to live a life guided by the Spirit of God. To do so allows us to please God, who has taken away our condemnation through the death and resurrection of Jesus Christ.

You may be wondering how this is possible. It's because the same Spirit that raised Jesus from the dead also dwells within us (8:11). This is our assurance. We are made alive in Christ, even as sin seeks to cause us to experience spiritual death. Our hearers should be encouraged that the power of the Resurrection is real and active today—in the here and now. Paul's theology of eschatology doesn't just yield to an experience of new life when we die, but he understands the freedom and liberation through Christ as something we are experiencing now.

This is also a matter of the mind. Paul is concerned about Christians having the mind of Christ and renewing our minds so that we can be led by the Spirit. He writes later in Romans 12:2, "Don't be conformed to the patterns of this world, but be transformed by the renewing of your minds so that you can figure out what God's will is—what is good and pleasing and mature." Paul is making a direct correlation with experiencing a life of peace and joy with keeping our minds on the Spirit. He writes in Romans 8:6 (ESV), "To set the mind on the flesh is death, but to set the mind on the Spirit is life and peace."

Bringing the Text to Life

In the spring of 2020, the world would be faced with a global health pandemic that would turn our lives upside down. There was unimaginable suffering because of COVID-19 and many turned to their faith for guidance and direction. In difficult times, we seek guidance from the Spirit of God because we have an assurance that God's presence remains near to us. Romans 8 is Paul providing readers with the everlasting assurance that, in Christ, we are not condemned; and through the Spirit, we can experience life and peace.

This text can challenge and encourage hearers at the same time. On one hand, it can challenge them to live a life led by the Spirit; and on the other hand, it can encourage them that their past sins have been forgiven. A few questions to consider: using stories from personal experience, how might you connect the good news of Christ with overcoming the guilt and shame many face because of sin? How can you explain the freedom from condemnation in a way that invites hearers to reflect on and rejoice in their personal relationship with Christ? What steps can they take to be formed spiritually in a new way?

Another avenue to explore with this text is the overwhelming amount of judgment people feel for a myriad of reasons. US gymnast Simone Biles experienced this during the 2020 Olympic Games in Tokyo. Biles was perhaps the most anticipated athlete to watch, but early in the games, she withdrew from each team event and all but one of her individual events due to mental-health concerns. Immediately, she received support from across the world, but also a wave of criticism and judgment. Most people will never know what it's like to be one of the most popular people on the planet, and how difficult it is to live up to the expectation to win at the highest levels of competition.

The connection that Simone Biles's story has with Romans 8 is that oftentimes people will judge and condemn without understanding the narrative of the person. And in Christ, we have a confidence that we can continue on our journey without condemnation. It liberates us from the guilt of not living up to other people's expectations. Millions were inspired by Simone Biles's resilience. She would eventually return for her final individual event and win the bronze medal.

The assurance that we have, even when others condemn, is that there is a freedom in knowing who you are. In Christ, you are a new creation. Therefore, the goal remains to set your mind on the Spirit who brings life and peace.

July 23, 2023–Eighth Sunday after Pentecost

Genesis 28:10-19a; Song of Solomon 12:13, 16-19; Isaiah 44:6-8;
Psalm 86:11-17; Psalm 139:1-12, 23-24; Romans 8:12-25;
Matthew 13:24-30, 36-43

Kevin Murriel

Preacher to Preacher Prayer

God of justice and truth, our world is filled with injustice and those who continue to plant seeds of division. There are also those who work tirelessly for justice who need your strength to continue standing up for the oppressed and those who are daily victims of systemic injustice. May you find us growing and continuing in the struggle for freedom, equity, and justice when you return with a harvest of truth and righteousness. In the liberating name of Jesus. Amen.

Commentary

Jesus would often tell parables using imagery that would be familiar to first-century listeners. Here, in Matthew 13:24-30, 36-43, Jesus uses sowing and harvesting. He is attempting to teach a spiritual lesson using a local example of a farmer who sowed good seed in his field, but while everyone slept, an enemy came and sowed weeds among the wheat. Immediately, one should question why someone would want to go through the trouble to sow weeds among the wheat. For the listeners, one could use this parable to give a unique perspective about evil in the world.

Greek word study is important here. Matthew uses the Greek term "zizania" for weeds, which, in that time, was known as "darnel." Darnel is a weed that most resembles wheat and in Israel, it would have been plentiful. The main way to tell the difference between wheat and darnel was for both to mature, when the ears of the real wheat would droop, while the ears of the darnel stood up straight. The harvesters would then come and separate the wheat and the weeds.

This parable calls us to watch the conditions of the world closely. There are many who sow good seeds in the earth, thinking that all the good that one does will yield a harvest of good; and it does. However, just as many are doing good, the enemy comes at unexpected moments and plants seeds of discord and disruption.

In this parable, those who are to gather the wheat are stunned to see weeds appearing in a field that should have only contained wheat. Of course, they are quick to want to pull up the weeds. They say, "'Master, didn't you plant good seed in your field? Then how is it that it has weeds?' 'An enemy has done this,' he answered. The servants said to him, 'Do you want us to go and gather them?' But the landowner said, 'No, because if you gather the weeds, you'll pull up the wheat along with them'" (13:27-29).

He then encourages them to "Let both grow side by side until the harvest. And at harvesttime I'll say to the harvesters, 'First gather the weeds and tie them together in bundles to be burned. But bring the wheat into my barn'" (13:30). Perhaps for the listeners, this text raises more questions than answers. Why does evil exist in the world? Why would God allow evil seeds to be planted among good? It is a deeper theological question of theodicy. Yet the text provides the assurance that after the harvest, "the righteous will shine like the sun in the kingdom of their Father" (13:43).

Bringing the Text to Life

Dr. Craig Hill was one of my favorite professors during my doctoral studies at Duke Divinity School. In his book *In God's Time: The Bible and the Future*, Dr. Hill's summary of all of eschatology is "God wins."[3] It is the affirmation that through the cosmic struggle between good and evil, our confidence is that good always prevails. In a time where injustice is pervasive, the words of Jesus provide comfort to those experiencing the sting of oppression. One could read and interpret this text through a social justice lens. The good seeds being planted are seeds of equity and equality for all people. The seeds that are sowed in the night by the enemy could represent those that attempt to keep people on the margins. Negative seeds such as health disparities, mass incarceration, income inequality, racism, gender-based violence, a lack of affordable housing, and many other justice issues could be focused on.

This text provides the preacher an opportunity to address many of the systemic evils of our world. As you examine this text through a social justice lens, how could your listeners be challenged in a different way? How could they respond differently to an interpretation of this text that calls them to action, and to continue to sow the "wheat" of justice despite the "weeds" of injustice that are planted?

A social justice interpretation of this text gives voice to those who have been victims of systemic injustice and challenges hearers not to ignore what's happening every day in our world. It is an opportunity to present Jesus as the one who connects to his proclamation in Luke 4:18-19: "The Spirit of the Lord is upon me, because the Lord has anointed me. He has sent me to preach good news to the poor, to proclaim release to the prisoners and recovery of sight to the blind, to liberate the oppressed, and to proclaim the year of the Lord's favor."

An interpretation of the Matthean parable that connects Christ's identity as Lord and Liberator to our call to keep growing in our pursuit of justice, despite the growth of systemic injustice, is relevant for today. This parable gives an appropriate response to how God will ultimately handle injustice in the end. As difficult as it may be to continue to work for justice when the weeds of injustice are so pervasive, the good news is that a harvest of truth and righteousness is coming.

July 30, 2023–Ninth Sunday after Pentecost

*Genesis 29:15-28; Psalm 105:1-11, 45b or Psalm 128; 1 Kings 3:5-12; Psalm 119:129-136; **Romans 8:26-39**; Matthew 13:31-33, 44-52*

Jeremy Squires

Preacher to Preacher Prayer

Thank you, Gracious God, that nothing at all can ever separate us from your amazing love and eternal grace, which is in Christ Jesus our Lord. Sometimes, we can imagine things that we have done or will do that can separate us from you, and yet your Word and the Word made flesh in Jesus clearly tells us that there is nothing that can hold back your love. Help me to accept this truth in my heart today, and never doubt your love for me. In Jesus's name I pray. Amen.

Commentary

The eighth chapter of Romans is so rich with meaning that we could easily find a series of sermons within it. The selected verses from Romans for this week are often read at a Celebration of Life to a grieving family and gathered community. They are found in Romans 8:31 and following where Paul finally comes to his main point through four different rhetorical questions: (1) Who can be against us, if God is for us? (2) Who will bring a charge against God's elect people? (3) Who is going to convict them? And the last one, which always speaks to me, (4) Who can separate us from the love of God?

The answer to all four questions is always the same. No one can come between God and us. Nothing can separate us from God's love. No one can be against us if God is for us. God will give us everything, since God already gave God's only Son for us. No one will bring any charge against God's elect, because God, the Creator of all the universe himself justifies us, pleads our case. No one can separate us from the love of God in Christ Jesus our Lord.

Even when it seems God has abandoned us, Paul writes in verse 35, we cannot escape his love. Paul quotes Psalm 44, a psalm of lament, to make his point. At a time when Israel felt that God had turned away forever, even then, God's love for his people could not be denied. Paul reassures us by proclaiming that we have seen the evidence of God's deep love for us in the person of Jesus. Paul says with conviction that we aren't forsaken but instead are victorious. In fact, we are more than conquerors through him who loved us.

What is this sweeping victory? Through Jesus, we can claim complete victory over the suffering caused by our sin. And what is the source of this victory? God's great love for us, shown in the death and resurrection of Jesus Christ. Once again, nothing can separate us from the love of God in Christ Jesus. Nothing.

Paul's final answer to the question, "Who will separate us from Christ's love?" is one of the most beautiful assurances we can find in scripture. "I'm convinced," Paul writes, "that nothing can separate us from the love of God in Christ Jesus our Lord: not death or life, not angels or rulers, not present things or future things, not powers or height or depth, or any other thing that is created." Paul makes a long list in this verse, but what if Paul were writing this promise today? What would make the list of things that cannot separate us from God's love? Maybe that is a question you can consider with your congregation.

Bringing the Text to Life

Shel Silverstein, author of *The Giving Tree*, wrote the children's poem "Whatif" that lists all the things a young child might fear, such as failure, disappointment, embarrassment, rejection, even death. "What if, what if, what if?" the poem asks.

Adults play the "What if" game, too. What if I had done this differently, or said that, or made a different decision? What if things go wrong and I can't fix them? One of my favorite comic book series by Marvel is called *What If?* It featured one or two stories about a Marvel superhero and what would have happened if they had made a different decision at a critical moment in their lives.

I wonder if this text makes our hearers want to ask the question, What If? when it comes to God's love. What if? What if I have done this or that? Will God still love me? Maybe you could actually play a What if? call-and-response game by having the congregation throw out what-ifs and then you respond, "Nothing can separate you from the love of God in Christ Jesus our Lord." Paul says let's stop "what if"-ing and rest in the assurance that we are more than conquerors through him who loved us. How can your congregation hear that truth this week?

August 6, 2023–Tenth Sunday after Pentecost

Genesis 32:22-31; Psalm 17:1-7, 15; Isaiah 55:1-5 or Psalm 145:8-9, 14-21; Romans 9:1-5; Matthew 14:13-21

Jeremy Squires

Preacher to Preacher Prayer

Lord, we have heard the story of Jacob wrestling with God and how he asked for you to bless him. We, too, come to you for blessing in the midst of our own spiritual wrestling. There are times in our lives in which we have felt alone and abandoned in the stillness of the dark night, waiting on you. But in those moments, you come and encourage us to stand strong. Be with us again, Almighty God, guide our lives, and help us receive your blessings. And, in turn, let us be a blessing to someone else. Amen.

Commentary

The story of Jacob, the "wounded wrestler," contains a host of material for preaching. There is the mystery of God being present in human form (incarnation anyone?). There is the wrestling match itself with all of its intimacy, closeness, and struggle. We can also dive deeper into identity and what winning a new name is all about for Jacob and us. I love this text and its possibilities because its meaning at every turn is not always very clear. So, let's wrestle with it too.

Jacob has heard that his brother, Esau, is coming to meet him, accompanied by four hundred men (32:6) to give him a little "welcome" party. Jacob's response is, of course, to panic (32:7), because he assumes Esau is coming to attack him as payback (32:8), which is probably not a bad assumption. Then Jacob prays to God for deliverance and tries to figure out how to buy some brotherly love.

Now Jacob is sending his wives and children across the river "Jabbok," which is related to the word *wrestle*. In Genesis 32:25, we find Jacob wrestling with his past. Later, while Jacob is alone, in the stillness of the night, at the ford of the Jabbok, an unidentified man literally wrestles with him. Who is this man? Maybe Jacob thought that Esau had caught him by surprise, or maybe Jacob had been half asleep and was confused. But, in his dreamlike state, Jacob wrestled with all the others with whom he had wrestled in his life, wrestling away the blessing from his father, Isaac, or wrestling away his wife, Rachel, from his father-in-law, Laban.

We don't know much about this wrestling match except that it lasted until right before the dawn's early light. At that time, the masked marvel of the universe or simply "he" sees it is a standstill and responds with a physical blow to Jacob's thigh or hip (32:32). The NIV says that he "touched" the socket of the hip. The CEB says he "grabbed" his thigh and tore a muscle. But the NRSV says that he "struck" him on the hip socket. Regardless of the force of the blow or the nature of the injury, Jacob refuses to relent.

Finally, in Genesis 32:26, his wrestling partner says "let me go because the dawn is breaking." We aren't told why this is important or needs to happen. Maybe it has something to do with Jacob seeing God during the daytime. Usually, God is in veiled form when being present with humanity. So maybe God is trying to protect him even as they wrestle.

Jacob refuses to stop wrestling until he receives a blessing, but the blessing doesn't happen immediately. Aren't there times in life when we are wrestling that we don't immediately see the "win" or the blessing?

In 32:27, we read that the man said to Jacob, "What's your name?" Most of us probably remember from seminary or Sunday school that Jacob's name has a variety of meanings including "supplanter," which is often interpreted as someone who seizes or circumvents.

Names are important to us, but in biblical times, they meant everything. They defined who someone was, their qualities, and their future. Needless to say, the name Jacob was not an encouraging one. However, God replies by doing two things: (1) giving Jacob a new name, Israel, and (2) pulling off his mask and identifying himself. Jacob, then, wants to know God's name, and he uses the magic word that in our house will always get you the best things in life. The word is "please" (32:29 NRSV).

But God is not finished yet and responds with a question, "Why is it that you ask my name?" If Jacob had an answer, we don't know it. Maybe it was in that moment that Jacob finally puts two and two together and gets the answer of "God." At that moment God blessed Jacob.

Bringing the Text to Life

What can we do to help our congregation learn from Jacob as he goes from grabber to wounded wrestler? Maybe we can admit that our way doesn't work. By crossing the Jabbok, Jacob would be entering the land that God has sworn to Abraham's descendants—the promised land. God wasn't about to allow Jacob to enter the land of God's blessing on his own terms or in his own strength.

And so, God appears in the form of a man and wrestles with Jacob in order to teach him some important truths. It appeared to be a draw until the man dislocated Jacob's hip with a simple touch. It was as if God allowed Jacob to give it his best shot, learning something about himself, and then God showed complete superiority with a single touch.

Although we may not enjoy such times, we too have our wrestling matches with God. Sometimes we wrestle with God over problems we don't understand or over God's will for our lives. Sometimes we wrestle with God because of questions that haunt us or, like Jacob, because of a deep desire for blessing. God wants us to persist and to engage. Jesus also talked about the power of persisting with God.

In 1849 a wagon train was traveling through Death Valley and as they looked ahead and saw a sheet of water, they all believed it was Owens Lake. But it was just a mirage created by the intense heat, and the harder they pressed on to make it to the water, the more frustrated they became. If we try to accomplish things in our own way and in our own strength, we will be just as frustrated as that wagon train pursuing a mirage. We will never be successful because our way simply doesn't work.

August 13, 2023–Eleventh Sunday after Pentecost

*Genesis 37:1-4, 12-28; Psalm 105:1-6, 16-22, 45b; **1 Kings 19:9-18**; Psalm 85:8-13; Romans 10:5-15; Matthew 14:22-33*

Jeremy Squires

Preacher to Preacher Prayer

O God, the One who provides, give us rest, and rejuvenate us in our own journey to a mountain of restoration—a mountain where we hear your call again, not in the powerful wind, frightening earthquake, or consuming fire but in your whisper. Let us find a place where we may hear you clearly and know you are near. We know that our waiting might be longer than we would like but we also know your timing is always perfect. Amen.

Commentary

In the nineteenth chapter of 1 Kings, we find Elijah at the lowest point in his life as a prophet. Ahab told Jezebel everything Elijah had done and how he had killed all the prophets with the sword. Jezebel vowed to kill Elijah and he ran for his life.

Elijah went a day's journey into the wilderness and sat down by a solitary broom tree, a symbol of his loneliness. He asked that he might die (v. 4), but an angel came to take care of him. Encouraged, Elijah journeyed forty days and forty nights to Horeb, the mount of God (v. 8). Pro tip: Don't lose sight of all the parallels here between Moses and Elijah (Exod 34). Elijah is literally walking the same path.

In the assigned text, we find Elijah in a cave sinking deeper and deeper into disbelief, listening to the words of Jezebel instead of Jehovah-Jireh. On Mount Carmel (1 Kgs 18), at the height of his career, he had boldly faced down the prophets of Jezebel, proclaiming the First Commandment. In our text he has now plummeted to the depths of his doubt on Mount Horeb (or Mount Sinai) and is no longer living that First Commandment. His god has become fear. Ultimately, this will become the story of transferring the call from a burned-out Elijah to a more willing servant Elisha.

Even while Elijah is holed up in the cave, God tries to reach him. Mount Horeb was a place of revelation for Moses and God hopes it will be for Elijah too. The Lord's word came to him and said, "Why are you here, Elijah?" (v. 9). Elijah complained to God that he had always served him with passion but his people weren't listening and they were destroying everything. "I'm the only one left, and now they want to take my life too!" (v. 10). And what does God do? "Go out and stand at the mountain before the Lord. The Lord is passing by" (v. 11). This seems rather strange until you consider what God might be up to. Have you ever been so down in the dumps, depressed, lost in the long night of the soul, that you couldn't even tell up from down or see the beauty in a beautiful day? And then something finally gets your attention?

God in verses 11-12 is attempting to move all of creation (wind, earthquake, and fire) and its power to shake Elijah out of the words of Jezebel and back into the words and power of God. God hopes that Elijah will snap out of it and remember who he is and whose he is.

Yet, it wasn't the awesome power of creation that moved Elijah. Instead, it was a whisper. "After the fire, there was a sound. Thin. Quiet." The NIV says a "gentle whisper" and the NRSV says it was the "sound of sheer silence." When Elijah heard it, he wrapped his face in his coat. He went out and stood at the cave's entrance (v. 13). A voice came to him again and asked, "Why are you here, Elijah?"

It is hard to believe, but Elijah's responses to God never change. Blinded by fear, Elijah is unable to see God's previous work on Mount Carmel and elsewhere in his life. His tunnel vision has led to a cave of no return. He clings to his fear of Jezebel's words rather than to God's promise. As a result, Elijah's life descends into an even darker place from fear into disobedience.

Even in his brokenness, Elijah was still a part of God's plans. God gives him three last instructions: (1) anoint Hazael as king of Aram, (2) anoint Jehu son of Nimshi as king of Israel, and (3) anoint Elisha as his replacement. Basically, these three will finish what Elijah started. However, Elijah only accomplishes one of these—the anointing of Elisha, who becomes his companion, and to whom he passes his mantle of being a prophet. It is Elisha in 2 Kings who commissions Hazael and anoints Jehu.

Bringing the Text to Life

Elijah's story is a cautionary and troubling tale that shows us one little word can fell us: fear. Fearful and faithless Elijah wouldn't go back and he couldn't move forward. He was paralyzed by his fear and he could no longer see or hear God. I think that was the reason why he got away from it all and went to Mount Horeb where Moses had encountered God.

Everybody loves vacations, right? It's our chance to get away, relax, and enjoy a different pace and space. Sometimes we get bogged down with the weight of our jobs and lives. Elijah was in the same place, at the end of his rope and needing time away with God. But God answered Elijah's concerns by calling him to go back the way he came. God reassured Elijah that he wasn't finished. Elijah was still part of God's plans.

When we need a break, the best thing we can do is rest and listen to God's voice for reassurance and then regroup. Elijah felt alone in the fight, but Elijah was never alone. God promises to never leave us (Heb 13:5). God's voice and presence are always with us. The challenge is being ready to listen and accept God's help in our times of trouble. Why are you here?

In the Nativity story, I remember this text being a lesson that the local teacher was teaching to the students. And she was walking through each part of it while the children were mesmerized and saying it with her. "But the Lord was not in the wind. But the Lord was not in the earthquake. But the Lord was not in the fire. And after the fire, there was a still small voice." How do we help our people focus and listen for the quiet voice of God in the midst of the chaos and noise of their fear and failings?

August 20, 2023–Twelfth Sunday after Pentecost

Genesis 45:1-15; Psalm 133; Romans 11:1-2a, 29-32; Matthew 15:(10-20), 21-28

Emily Hotho

Preacher to Preacher Prayer

God who works all things together for good, be present in my study and preparation. God who has reconciled us to yourself through the cross of Christ, help me to reflect on the needs for forgiveness and reconciliation in my relationships, community, and world. Amen.

Commentary

The previous week's lectionary reading introduced us to Joseph as a young boy. Today's reading picks up the narrative toward the end of Joseph's story; he reveals himself to his brothers who sold him into slavery all those years ago. Consider whether your audience is familiar enough with the Joseph narrative to fill in the gaps between those two texts, or whether your message might need to include a brief summary of Joseph's time in Potiphar's house, his time in prison, and his rise to power in Pharaoh's service.

Many hearers will connect with the themes of repentance, forgiveness, and reconciliation in this passage. After all, the emotion in this scene is vivid and palpable. Twice in this text, and five times in the final five chapters of Genesis, Joseph is described as "weeping." It is notable that we don't see Joseph weep when he's sold into slavery, nor when he is wrongly accused by Potiphar's wife, nor when he is forgotten and alone in prison. But in this final piece of Joseph's story, he weeps loudly, openly, and often. Nothing Joseph went through was as emotionally hard for him as wrestling with forgiveness and reconciliation.

It is also important to connect this scene with the one in Genesis 50:15-21. In Genesis 45, Joseph is making theological sense of what happened to him. The restoring of Joseph's relationships with his brothers comes later. Forgiveness is a journey, not an instantaneous occurrence, a truth to which our hearers can surely relate.

This text also raises the question of theodicy, the notion of divine goodness in view of the existence of evil. From chapters 37 to 44 of Genesis, God's name is hardly mentioned as Joseph's journey unfolds. But in today's reading, Joseph assigns ultimate responsibility for what happened to him to God. Notice how many times Joseph echoes, "God sent me here . . ." "God made me master of Egypt . . ."

We must wrestle with the issue that it was, indeed, Joseph's brothers who plotted to kill him and then settled for selling him into slavery. We must wrestle with the reality of slavery itself. Did a good and loving God really cause such evil, all for the sake of getting the Hebrew people to Egypt to survive the famine? Such an interpretation is as theologically problematic as saying that God gave someone cancer in order to teach that person a lesson, or that someone died because God needed another angel in heaven. A more helpful interpretation may be that divine agency and human agency are both at work. Joseph's brothers had evil purposes and committed evil actions. Slavery itself is an evil institution. But even in the midst of evil, God was working for ultimate good.

There's no better example of God using evil for good than the cross of Jesus. Scholars have noted that Joseph's story seems to foreshadow Jesus's story. Joseph was sold for twenty shekels by Judah; Jesus was sold for thirty pieces of silver by Judas. They were both hated by people around them, but sent by God to save. Matthew Henry wrote, "Joseph was here a type of Christ. Though he was the beloved Son of his Father, and hated by a wicked world, yet the Father sent him out of his bosom to visit us . . . he came from heaven to earth, to seek and save us."[1]

Bringing the Text to Life

With a narrative text like this one, let the story shine. Retell the story of Joseph in your own words, or even reimagine it in a modern context. Look to popular depictions of the Joseph story in art, music, and drama, such as Andrew Lloyd Weber's *Joseph and the Amazing Technicolor Dreamcoat*, and notice what parts of Joseph's story their interpretations highlight.

The preacher might also explore modern-day examples of forgiveness and reconciliation. In 1993, a young, white woman named Amy Biehl, a Fulbright scholar working with poor communities in apartheid South Africa, was violently murdered by four black youths. Her parents, despite their grief and anger, were able to come to understand that the systemic evil of apartheid created the conditions that led to the personal evil of their daughter's murder. They eventually even hired two of the young men who killed Amy to work in a foundation they set up in their daughter's name. The Biehl family has written and spoken extensively on forgiveness, reconciliation, and restorative justice. Like the Joseph story, this story touches on theodicy as well; God did not cause Amy's murder, and God did not orchestrate apartheid, but God was working even in the midst of evil to bring about something good.

Preaching about forgiveness and reconciliation can present challenges, especially when we consider how our general theological statements might be applied to someone in a situation of domestic violence or abuse. Choose words and examples with care, making clear that forgiveness does not always mean continuing a relationship, especially one that is harmful.

Seeing God's good work in the midst of evil can help our listeners take steps toward forgiveness. Consider current situations within the congregation, community, or world in which we might look for how God has been working for good, and thus open our hearts to the possibility of forgiveness and reconciliation.

August 27, 2023–Thirteenth Sunday after Pentecost

Exodus 1:8–2:10; Psalm 124; **Romans 12:1-8**; *Matthew 16:13-20*

Emily Hotho

Preacher to Preacher Prayer

Dear God, thank you for the measure of faith and the spiritual gifts that have been given to me, and to each person in my community. Together, preacher and congregation, help us to discern how you are calling us to be transformed and renewed as living sacrifices to your glory, and to share our gifts humbly with one another and the world. Amen.

Commentary

Many of Paul's letters were to churches he had personally founded, and they address specific issues within those churches. Not so with Romans; Paul didn't establish the Roman church. He hadn't even met them yet. But we learn from the opening verses of the letter that he hoped to visit them soon. Later in Romans (chapter 15), we find that Paul planned to extend his missionary efforts westward to Spain, and that he hoped the Roman church would assist him in that mission. And so he sent this letter spelling out his teachings, so the Roman Christians could come to know, understand, and support this apostle whom they'd never met.

The early chapters of Romans teach the doctrines of sin, justification by faith in Jesus, and new life in the Spirit. Chapters 9-11 explain how Jesus fulfilled God's promises to Israel, and how, although Paul hopes his Jewish siblings will eventually come to know Christ, he also believes God will not abandon those who remain faithful to Judaism, either.

Romans 12:1 (NIV) begins with the word *therefore*. Whenever we see "therefore" in the text, we ask ourselves "What's it there for?" The word is typically a link between the concept that has come before, and the one that is about to come next.

Therefore, in light of salvation by faith, in light of God's mercy toward Jews and Christians alike, Paul urges his readers to "present your bodies as a living sacrifice that is holy and pleasing to God" (v. 2 CEB). Knowing that the previous section of Romans focused on Judaism makes the sacrificial overtones of this verse crystal clear. Just as sacrifices were presented on the altar of the Jerusalem temple, we are called to present our entire selves as living sacrifices given in worship to God. Paul is saying that worshipping God with our whole lives is the true worship to which Judaism has always pointed.

Verse 2 also hearkens back to the Jewish understanding of a present age, and a new age to come. Although the CEB and many other translations use the term "world," the Greek is *aioni* (as in *eon*, meaning age). We live in the tension between the present and the new, the already and the not-yet. Paul urges his readers not to be conformed to the present age, but to be transformed and renewed, ready for the new day that has dawned in Christ.

Verses 3-8 show us more of the ethical implications of the theology Paul has taught thus far in Romans. Because of God's grace, we ought to live with humility and use our gifts for the common good. Paul's body imagery and list of spiritual gifts is similar to 1 Corinthians 12, emphasizing that unity does not require uniformity, and that there are no insignificant parts within the body of Christ.

Bringing the Text to Life

Augustine of Hippo, Martin Luther, and John Wesley all trace their spiritual awakenings to the book of Romans. Perhaps this is because it presents the gospel in such a clear and logical way, and because it includes not only the theological but the ethical implications of how Christianity is meant to transform and renew us. A preacher might want to explore these stories of spiritual renewal rooted in Romans and perhaps even retell one in your own words.

You might also consider illustrations from among your own community. Is there someone who has chosen not to conform, but to be transformed, as a means of worshipping God with their whole life?

Or, focusing on verses 3 through 8 of the text, you may want to lift up persons in your congregation with different gifts who use them with humility for the common good. This can be a wonderful opportunity to highlight behind-the-scenes servants while also illustrating the text.

If this is a Communion Sunday in your congregation, the Communion liturgy offers a logical tie-in with the text: "we offer ourselves in praise and thanksgiving as a holy and living sacrifice, in union with Christ's offering for us."[2] We say these words each week or each month, without always considering their implications for our lives.

Fred Craddock gave this illustration:

> We think giving our all to the Lord is like taking a $1,000 bill and laying it on the table—"Here's my life, Lord. I'm giving it all."
>
> But the reality for most of us is that he sends us to the bank and has us cash in the $1,000 for quarters. We go through life putting out 25 cents here and 50 cents there. Listen to the neighbor kid's troubles instead of saying, "Get lost." Go to a committee meeting. Give up a cup of water to a shaky old man in a nursing home.
>
> Usually giving our life to Christ isn't glorious. It's done in all those little acts of love, 25 cents at a time. It would be easy to go out in a flash of glory; it's harder to live the Christian life little by little over the long haul.[3]

September 3, 2023– Fourteenth Sunday after Pentecost

Exodus 3:1-15; Psalm 105:1-6, 23-26, 45b; Romans 12:9-21;
Matthew 16:21-28

Emily Hotho

Preacher to Preacher Prayer

O God, at times I am, like Peter, a stumbling block. But my desire is to be a rock on whom you can build your church. Help me to resist evaluating everything by human measures of success and glory, and instead take up my cross and follow you. Amen.

Commentary

This text is a sequel to last week's gospel reading. Matthew has contained our Gospel reading throughout this season after Pentecost, and last week, we saw Peter declare Jesus the Messiah, the Son of the living God, to which Jesus responded, "You are Peter. And I'll build my church on this rock. The gates of the underworld won't be able to stand against it" (Matt 16:18).

But in today's reading, things don't go quite as well for Peter. Jesus begins to explain to his disciples that he will soon have to suffer and die. Notice how Peter responds. Taking hold of Jesus. Scolding him! Correcting him: "God forbid, Lord!" Peter's intense response reflects an incomplete understanding of Jesus's mission, but also a deep personal love for Jesus, as well as the passionate personality he displays elsewhere in the Gospels.

Jesus's reply to Peter seems strange, even harsh. "Get behind me, Satan. You are a stone that could make me stumble" (vv. 22-23). But Jesus wasn't calling his friend and disciple "Satan" as an insult. "Satan" means "adversary," and Peter was acting adversarial to Jesus's purpose. Peter wanted Jesus to rise to power rather than carry a cross. He had fallen victim to the same temptations that Satan presented to Jesus in Matthew 4, which Henri Nouwen crystallized as the temptations to be relevant, popular, and powerful.[1]

Notice also the connection between Peter being called a "rock" a few verses prior, and a "stumbling block" here. Rocks can be powerful, strong, and useful. But they can also be stubborn, immovable, and can get in the way. Jesus seems to be intentionally choosing a play on words by juxtaposing these two phrases.

The direction for Peter to "get behind" Jesus is not just a posture of submission, it is a posture of discipleship; the Greek word for "behind" is the same as the word *follow* as in Jesus's call, "Come, follow me."

Jesus seems to be challenging Peter to follow him in the way of self-giving love. This is made clear in verses 24-28, which Jesus addresses to the entire group of disciples, encouraging them, and all of us, to take up our individual crosses and even be willing to lose our lives in pursuit of following Jesus.

Bringing the Text to Life

A lighthearted introduction to the message could feature the 1950s board game for Christian families called "Going to Jerusalem." The playing pieces were tiny plastic disciples with robes, beards, and sandals. Players would move across the board, starting in Bethlehem, rolling dice and looking up corresponding Bible verses. If you rolled the dice well, you went all the way to the triumphal entry into Jerusalem, and there were no demons or angry Pharisees hindering you. You also never got to Jesus's arrest, trial, or crucifixion if your path took you this way. It was a safe adventure through the nice stories, culminating in a Palm Sunday parade. Peter, too, was eager to follow Jesus to places of power, but he was surprised when Jesus called him to places of suffering instead.

The imagery in the text of rocks and stumbling stones lends itself well to visual illustration. This scene takes place in Caesarea Philippi, an outlier location from the rest of Jesus's ministry. Caesarea Philippi was built near a spring that gushes from a massive rock, surrounded by caves and steep cliffs. It is here that Jesus calls Peter both a rock and a stumbling stone. Consider creative use of rocks or stones in the worship service by showing them on the altar or on projection screens, or even distributing a small rock to each worshipper to serve as a reminder of this message.

Peter didn't understand yet that Jesus wasn't building a palace in Jerusalem. Jesus wasn't building a mansion of glory for when they conquered the Romans. That's what Peter had been hoping for and expecting. So, when Jesus said he was going to suffer on a cross and die, Peter just couldn't believe it. Jesus is building a church that is founded on death and resurrection. Jesus is building his church, his way, and we are the stones he wants to use (1 Pet 2:5).

You might also consider examples from your own life of times when you've been eager to follow Jesus to places of power but not to places of suffering, or stories from your own community in which someone has taken up their cross faithfully.

September 10, 2023– Fifteenth Sunday after Pentecost

Exodus 12:1-14; Psalm 149; Ezekiel 33:7-11; Psalm 119:33-40;
*Romans 13:8-14; **Matthew 18:15-20***

Mandy Sloan McDow

Preacher to Preacher Prayer

Draw us in the Spirit's tether, for when humbly in Thy name, two or three are met together
Thou art in the midst of them. Alleluia! Alleluia Almighty God, give us the courage we
need to address those who have wronged us, and give us grace to confess our fault when we
are in the wrong. Amen.

Commentary

I grew up in a moderate-sized mainline Protestant church in East Tennessee. When I was a child, the church was filled with people who became my mentors, teachers, babysitters, and very best friends. As I grew up, the youth group would perpetually wax and wane in size. Conflicting sports schedules, personalities, and changing priorities made Sunday evenings a challenging time to trek across town for two hours of programming and pizza. There were nights, especially in the heat of summer, when our group—which typically numbered around twenty people—fell to a modest two to three. Inevitably, a good-hearted volunteer would slide a piece of Mr. Gatti's pizza onto a thin paper plate and remind the handful of us in attendance: "Where two or three are gathered, God is in their midst!" and then quietly return the extra two liters of RC Cola to the refrigerator for next week.

Growing up, I assumed this scripture was meant for small youth groups and prayer partners. The author of "Draw us in the Spirit's Tether" agrees with me, penning the comforting verse: "Draw us in the Spirit's tether, for when humbly in thy name, two or three are met together, thou art in the midst of them. Alleluia! Alleluia!

Touch we now thy garment's hem."[2] It has only been since entering pastoral ministry that this text became more vibrant and interesting.

In this pericope, Jesus speaks, not to comfort the hearts of those who expected more people to attend their gathering, but to what should happen when a member of the church sins against another. I was shocked to learn that this passage was about conflict management, and grateful that Jesus offers such clear instructions for a circumstance that often brings out the worst in people. Jesus says that in our conflict, we are to approach one another, speak with truth and compassion, and let the other know how they have wronged us. If he will not listen, then we try again and bring an elder of the church. For, Jesus said, "For where two or three are gathered in my name, I'm there with them" (v. 20). This notion of God being present in the smallest of congregations is not just comfort to tiny churches, it is a promise that when two or three are gathered to work out a conflict, God will be in the midst of them.

The best part of this text is something we usually discard as we read it. Jesus says, "If the one who sins against you will not listen, treat them as you would a Gentile or tax collector." It is easy to hear this as permission to dismiss those who are reluctant to see the error of their ways; after all, Gentiles and tax collectors were hardly considered good company in Jesus's day. Except that Jesus doesn't keep company with the "good" ones: the church-goers, the faithful, the Pharisees or Sadducees. Rather, he relentlessly sought out and welcomed the marginalized and shunned, the Gentiles and tax collectors. This encourages us to always reach out in love, especially to those who are difficult, unrepentant, and beyond hope. This is Jesus instructing us to forgive, not seven times seven, but seventy times seven . . . for as long as it takes.

Bringing the Text to Life

There is a microcosm of this opportunity in our worship services. Most Communion liturgies begin with the invitation to confess our sins, and to forgive those who have sinned against us. When we gather for Holy Communion, we are invited to receive God's grace as we feast at a small table. We are also reminded that this table extends into every church where Christ's name is praised. This is a gorgeous sentiment. But, we give little thought to the understanding that when we gather at this table, we'll be joined by folks who *don't* like us. And we don't like them. We'll be dining with those who hate and misunderstand us, who have sinned against us, and think that we have no right to be at that table. And, we may think the same of them.

It is through a loving and merciful God that people who deeply misunderstand one another can come and sit and eat with the same sense of grace and peace. We pray, at the setting of the table, "As disciples used to gather, In the name of Christ to sup, Then with thanks to God the Father. Break the bread and bless the cup, Alleluia! Alleluia! So, knit thou our friendship up." It is easy to think of being knit together with people we love, and people who love us. But, what are we to do with the folks who don't? Communion Sunday forces the issue.

When receiving the sacrament, sinners of all sorts (ourselves included) will find the face of Jesus in this moment of partaking. And, friends, it is up to us to see the face of Christ in all of those who are humble enough to gather at this table. For, not one who approaches comes without the mark of suffering on her brow. In the sacrament, we feast with Job, who lost everything except his ability to praise God. We feast with denominations who are still seeking to understand how to be welcoming and accepting. We feast with your grandmother who always loved you, and your uncle who always misunderstood you. We feast with your neighbor, and with the bully from fourth grade. Praise God, we will even feast with our over-the-top friend, taken from us too soon, who shall wait for us at Jesus's right hand with a dirty martini, poured to perfection.

We have all sinned and fallen short of the glory of God, and we have all forsaken our promises to be kind, gracious, forgiving, merciful. We have made assumptions about others, without knowing their stories, their wounds. And, in the sacrament of Communion, we are invited to eat together at this holy table, bringing our sufferings, our struggles, our fears. We will lay them down, for we are all promised the same love that can only come from God, as we are bound together by the Holy Spirit: *"All our meals and all our living, make as sacraments of thee, That by caring, helping, giving, We may true disciples be. Alleluia! Alleluia! We will serve thee faithfully."*

September 17, 2023– Sixteenth Sunday after Pentecost

Exodus 14:19-31; Psalm 114; Genesis 50:15-21;
Psalm 103:(1-7), 8-13; Romans 14:1-12; Matthew 18:21-35

Mandy Sloan McDow

Preacher to Preacher Prayer

Almighty God, you are a God of justice and a God of grace. Help us to see the long arc of your steadfast love as we seek to understand your mercy. Amen.

Commentary

This is a story of resurrection. It is as critical to the Hebrew Bible as the Easter story is to the Gospels. This is the story of the Israelites' gift of new life, free from slavery and death, and the beginning of their journey to the promised land. But, before it is a story of resurrection, it is a story of death and destruction. This is a difficult text to preach because it says things about a grace-filled, loving God that seem deeply counter to our experience with faith. This God is hard to sell. This God is, sometimes, too easy to find. This God destroys the Egyptians by swallowing them up in the sea, only to bring the Israelites into decades of wilderness living. It's a story that doesn't play well with history or science, and it certainly doesn't appeal to our sense of God's mercy. It paints a picture of a punitive God, prone to judgment and wrath. This God is hard to preach.

But it is also difficult to preach resurrection when death is still walking among us. Every year, I sit down and look through the photos and stories from September 11, 2001, because that day divides our history as an American citizen into a before and after. I was beginning my second year of seminary, and I watched and listened as our professors struggled to find God in the airplanes, burning buildings, and collapsed towers. Some were able to do so, giving God the grace to be present in horrific situations. Some were angrier than they'd ever been, railing against a God who, they believed, was definitely absent on that day. We sat in classrooms with faithful people who tried their best to make theological sense of the day, and we became a postmodern, post-9/11 group of pastors who could no longer take a beautiful, late summer Tuesday for granted.

And death is still here with us, making fools of the folks like me who believe strongly in resurrection. As I write, we are still deep in the midst of the COVID-19 pandemic. Our world has changed, and we have lost so many people whom we love. We have done countless funerals in virtual settings, comforted the grieving, and prayed that our congregations would find a way to survive. We do not have the luxury of ignoring our mortality, and even if we believe that one's spirit cannot be contained in this life, and will never cease to be, it is hard to argue with the power of death's seeming finality.

Just as the central story of Jesus's death and resurrection comes to us in four different versions, so the central story of the Israelites' exodus and the Red Sea event comes to us in three different versions that have been woven together and placed alongside one another.[3] In each version, there is a different emphasis on who is doing the action. In verse 14 (NRSV), Moses instructs the Israelites that "the LORD will fight for you, and you have only to keep still." But in verses 20-21, Moses extends his hand over the sea, and the Lord drives the sea back by a strong wind and turned the water into dry ground, and it was then that the Israelites walked through the sea, with walls of water on either side. These versions emphasize different ways for us to interpret our own faith. On one hand, we are asked to be still, to wait on God, who will fight for us. On the other hand, we are asked to *do* something, because this is our response to God's witness in our life.

Bringing the Text to Life

Contending with God's willingness to allow (and in this case, endorse) bad things to happen to people is a task that will last a lifetime. Benyamin Cohen writes,

> The Jewish nation had just witnessed a dramatic turn of events. One moment they were ready to admit defeat and return to Egypt, and the next, they were miraculously saved. It was at this precise moment, when disaster seemed inevitable, that calamity was changed into hope, promise, and faith. Their spirits had been exalted. It was at this moment, that the Jews burst into song to praise their redeemer, their creator. They chose to show their gratitude through the universal language of song.[4]

But, for me, I have a more skeptical view of this singular event, because I know what follows it: a season of wandering in the wilderness and the need for commandments, with angry people who are hungry and isolated. And, yet. God remains steadfast. There is direction and provision. There is a reluctant leader who never fails. There is provision of manna and water from a rock. There is restoration in the promised land. My dear rabbi friend reminds me that he is able to celebrate because of the singular day that marked the sign of God's promise for all. But, I need to slog through the rest of the story to find the grace and redemption.

And yet, God knows that. God has given us all the ability to take our doubt and our need and our lack of full understanding and hold it tightly, because God can do things greater than we can perceive. God can demonstrate grace, even through destruction. God can offer salvation, even through a crucified messiah. God can defeat death, through the promise of resurrection. This is our hope. This is our promise. This is our story. This is our song. Let us never stop singing it together.

September 24, 2023– Seventeenth Sunday after Pentecost

Exodus 16:2-15; Psalm 105:1-6, 37-45; Jonah 3:10-4:11;
*Psalm 145:1-8; Philippians 1:21-30; **Matthew 20:1-16***

Mandy Sloan McDow

Preacher to Preacher Prayer

God of compassion and justice, help us to see the world as you do through the lens of love, rather than the lens of fairness. Amen.

Commentary

The text for today follows Jesus's encounter with the rich, young man who was invited to be a disciple, but was too beholden to his possessions to sell them. Peter is immediately concerned, because he is the Barney Fife of the disciples. Peter's dual natures, unchangeably, indivisibly, and inseparably are enthusiasm and foolishness. Never one to disappoint Jesus, Peter asks what the disciples will get because they *did* leave everything to follow him. I wish there was a comparable word to *Selah* for when Jesus has *had it* with people, because you can almost hear a despondent sigh as he reminds his earnest and beloved disciple that he will receive a throne, where he will sit in judgment over one of the twelve tribes of Israel, a hundredfold of what he has left behind, *and* eternal life. If that isn't enough for Peter's comfort, Jesus concludes with: "So those who are last will be first. And those who are first will be last" (v. 16).

Jesus, knowing that this will need some explanation, takes this opportunity to share the parable of the laborers in the vineyard. To begin, I want to honor the scholarship of Amy-Jill Levine, a Jewish scholar who specializes in New Testament studies. The customary read on this parable as an allegory describing the landlord as God who chides the children of Israel while seeking to welcome the Gentiles is troubling. Levine advises, "When Jewish practice or Jewish society becomes the negative foil to Jesus or the church, we do well to re-read the parable."[5]

An allegorical reading only separates Jesus from his Jewish context, which doesn't serve to advance the discussion of how the last could be first.

Rather than debate who the laborers and landowner symbolically represent, it seems more compelling to ask, who is in the vineyard, and who is missing? Quite simply, who has been hired, and why?

The laborers who are hired first seem to have no distinguishing characteristics or special skills. They were simply hired first, based on rationale that made sense to the landowner. He agreed to the usual daily wage: the denarius of the day. This is the token of one's industry, the proof of economic exchange for services rendered.

While saying nothing about *why* the first workers are hired, Jesus goes into great detail to tell us the exact times that the landowner returns to the marketplace to hire additional laborers. At the end of the day, each worker is paid the same amount. The workers hired first begin to grumble, because they worked all day in the scorching heat, and the workers hired last only worked an hour.

The issue that quickly surfaces is the problem that economic abundance undermines the basic principle of capitalism. "Work" has been used as a weapon against the class system, to tell those in lower-income brackets that they are to work harder in order to pull out of poverty (as if poverty can be overcome by sheer will alone).

When the Landowner (the Lord) pays everyone the same wage, he cuts at the heart of the capitalist system. "Work" doesn't make one wealthy, but *opportunity* can. He is right to say, "I did you no wrong . . . are you resentful because I'm generous?"

The answer, of course, is yes. Generosity isn't rewarded in capitalism.

It is easy to understand that the laborers all want the same thing: to be paid for their labor, and to provide for their families. They all receive the denarius of the day, and are able to do so. The curiosity is why this causes the first workers to grumble. Equal compensation for all takes nothing away from the industry or provision of the workers who arrived first. So, what is it they really want? Is it to be paid fairly? Or, do they want to maintain the scalable economic system that affirms that their labor has more value than those who were hired last.

Consider this: how much time have you spent studying the theology of Augustine, Wesley, and Barth, and how little time have you devoted to James Cone, Renita Weems, and Wil Gafney? The first were first because . . . they were first. Their work is the foundation of Christian thought, but their work does not speak to the sum total of the human experience. How depressing would it be if all of the good work had already been done? As it happens, there is always plenty of work to do.

Bringing the Text to Life

As the pandemic raged worldwide, the sins of our nation exposed themselves like Adam and Eve in the garden. No fig leaf is capable of hiding the shameful hold that white supremacy has over our country. Not a single moment of America's history exists outside of the propaganda of Manifest Destiny and the desire to assert the value of white, European lives over others. Indigenous tribes, enslaved Africans, and non-white immigrants have lived too long as the day laborers, serving the landowner, the plantation, the cotton lord.

What the world tells us is that our industry has value, because it propels the motor of the capitalist machine. What the gospel tells us is that our generosity has even more value. Rather than grumbling that everyone has enough, we should rejoice. In generosity, capitalism loses its power.

All of us have felt the tug of injustice, the sting of unfairness. What I find so compelling about this parable is that it *is* fair. And yet, fairness isn't satisfactory.

So, what is Jesus trying to teach us here? Remember, we have just heard Jesus say that it's harder for a rich man to enter the kingdom of heaven than it is for a camel to pass through the eye of a needle. He also told Peter, who asked what the disciples would get for giving up everything, the "last will be first" (v. 16).

I would offer that we haven't yet considered the workload of the laborers who were hired early in the morning. They were hired to tend to the vineyard, which is likely large and exhausting work, especially in the heat of day. As the day draws on, the landowner, who does not seem to need additional help, continues back to the marketplace to hire more workers. As he does so, the burden of labor is lightened. With each additional person who arrives, the amount for each worker to accomplish is lessened. "Many hands make for light work," after all.

If it is true that the yoke is heavy, but the burden is light, then that means the landowner knew that his ask was significant. The work to be accomplished could be done with a few, but hiring more workers meant that the job could be completed in a day, and with a lighter workload for each person. The only way to bear a heavy burden is to share it. The landowner isn't just generous, he's compassionate.

Biblical economic justice isn't about hourly wages, but about equal access to the means necessary to participate in a consumer-based system. Stanley Sunders writes that this passage directly addresses the plight of day laborers as a "limitless and disposable fuel . . . [who] never gain enough traction to be able to join the world of consumers."[6]

Much like love, the resources in this parable are not finite. There is enough to go around, so that everyone has what they need. All God asks in return is our faithfulness to believe it.

October 1, 2023– Eighteenth Sunday after Pentecost

Exodus 17:1-7; Psalm 78:1-4, 12-16; Philippians 2:1-13; Matthew 21:23-32

Roland Millington

Preacher to Preacher Prayer

Dear Lord, I pray for my brothers and sisters as they bring to light a closer fullness that waits for us in your word.

Commentary

Exodus 17:1 begins by foreshadowing the bookend of Exodus 17:7. Israel means "strives with God," and the location where this event occurs is Massah and Meribah, the place of rebellion and strife. Going against God will often lead to rebellion and strife. In Exodus 17:2, the people quarrel with Moses, their figurehead and go-between with Yahweh. This perplexed Moses as he was already convinced of the power of God to provide and work wonders.

Exodus 17:3 shows us people desperately thirsty for water. To them, the wilderness was a frightening place, and death lurked at their tent door. They were visibly desperate, and Moses took his request to God, realizing just how alarming the situation had become (Exod 17:4). Note that the people went to Moses with claims of malfeasance, but Moses went directly to God with a request for instructions: the difference between faith and floundering. God proceeds to give Moses instructions to go before all the people and bring some elders along with him. Moses followed God's instruction, striking the rock so that water would come out (*veyatzeyu*). Moses does as God commands, and the water comes forth, giving the people another miracle. This passage holds a repeated pattern that would emerge throughout their history, especially apparent after Joshua in the Judges time line. The cycle of disbelief, sin, oppression, repentance, deliverance, and peace was continual with them, as it is with us.

The inability to find order appears to be a common difficulty.

When we think of an ordered and structured world, we often associate that with structure, which is most closely associated with nonorganic shapes. Buildings, bridges, monuments, and houses all evoke a sense of pattern and order. To Abraham, this was not the case. Nevertheless, to his progeny coming out of Egypt, it most certainly was.

The story we find in Exodus 17:1-7 is of God's reintroduction to the former slaves fleeing Egypt. It is a story inclusive of absolute panic and reading it should emphasize this. The scene is the dusty and dry wilderness where a hardscrabble existence awaits the former slaves. The problem is that their lives revolved around the structure of production. The cycle to which they were accustomed involved making bricks, placing them in a prescribed pattern until the manufactured pattern was completed, and then moving to the next project. The only rhythm they knew was pain, exhaustion, and labor, from sunup to sundown. The bricks they made would change in shape and number, the patterns would deviate somewhat, and the projects were ever changing at the whim of the builders.

To the ancestors of these slaves, the wilderness was the only place order existed. This is because the Abrahamic people before the exodus were agrarian, relying on crops and livestock in a cycle of planting and harvest, birth and death. Our Western concept of immortality, one consciousness carrying forward forever, was not the same as theirs. Their idea of immortality came from the seed, and we see it expressed in the pictographic alphabet used at the time. The letter that would eventually go from Semitic script to Greek to Roman and finally to our modern letter *n* is the Hebrew pictograph for a seed with a seed head (*nun*) was coupled with the pictographic Hebrew letter for the tent, which became our letter *b* (*beit*). Together these two mean "seed of the house" or "son." We pronounce them "ben."

If the alphabet of these early people was not enough proof of order in the wilderness, we could also find clues to this in scripture. It appears in psalms about nature (Pss 8:3-4; 96:11-12; Ps 145:5) to Job's admonishment to seek knowledge of God through nature. Cities were often places of ill repute, dark and shadowy, but the wilderness was a place where one might find God's provision.

This passage from Exodus feels familiar to us because the former slaves had a mindset similar to ours of today. They felt that water should come from a well and that life flourished in cities where they relied on the human provision. Moses showing the power of God by obediently striking the rock and seeing water gush forth for the people who would become the nation of Israel was important. For us, it marks a clear delineation between where we think we find God and where we do find God.

The quarreling as to whether or not God was with the people did not die. The cyclical nature of turning away from the will of God continued to be an issue for the people destined to be the kingdom of Israel. This is not something that will end, either, as we find in Zechariah 14:16-19, where even though God's presence has returned to Jerusalem, some will pay the price for not worshipping there. Some still choose not to acknowledge divine provision.

Bringing the Text to Life

It is fitting to bring concepts people understand, the most readily available ones being camping or going back to the wilderness. Having to rely on things put in place for us by God requires reorienting ourselves to think of nature as a friend and not a foe. Older congregations might benefit from recalling the television show *The Life and Times of Grizzly Adams*, where a man left the world behind to find harmony in nature.

It is a good idea to connect this to burgeoning interests in spirituality, whether one uses the idea of Celtic "thin spaces," scientific (yet divinely ordered) structures in ecosystems, or even scriptural connections such as Micah 6:8. Note that the words we translate as "seek justice" translated more accurately as "seek order."

October 8, 2023– Nineteenth Sunday after Pentecost

*Exodus 20:1-4, 7-9, 12-20; Psalm 19; Philippians 3:4b-14;
Matthew 21:33-46*

Roland Millington

Preacher to Preacher Prayer

Lord God, move your Holy Spirit within the hearts of my sisters and brothers to bring a message of significant personal change and interpersonal growth in the congregation they serve.

Commentary

When we speak of these passages, we often come at them from a highly traditional standpoint, meaning "What was preached initially must still be good." The issue with never going back to the original languages is that we often miss what has changed in linguistics and archaeology since some of the earliest commentaries. Taking a fresh look at the scripture and adjusting our lenses to contemporary discoveries can give us a much sharper focus on scripture. This need is quite evident in these passages from Exodus.

Exodus 20:1—God is speaking all these words, meaning what follows is the literal word of God. The text then goes on to state that it was God who brought the people out of Egypt, and out of slavery (*ebedim*, slavery). Comparatively, this is interesting because later in Joshua, we find the command to fear God and serve (*abad*, serve as a slave) him. God has laid claim to the people explicitly for God's purpose. The command sets God's purpose and place in the hierarchy of our lives ahead of anything else that we may consider important (Exod 20:3). At face value, the people of the exodus were trading one slave master for another. You can begin to see why the people grumbled against Moses and Aaron here. Perhaps they felt duped, as they had not delved deep enough into the character of God. We would say their faith was small and fragile because the inbirthed persuasion of God (faith) had not fully formed in them.

Exodus 20:4 tells us that God's command states there must be no carved images made of anything in heaven, on earth, in the sea, or below the earth. We have an issue with this: God then appears to instruct Moses to break this commandment in Numbers 21:8 (the serpent staff) and Exodus 25:18 (Cherubim on the ark). Again, more incongruence on the surface, but when read with Exodus 20:5, we see the prohibition clarified concerning the worship of these things, not necessarily possession or creation. Purpose and place are essential.

Exodus 20:7 brings us to the point. The command not to take God's name in vain. Many understand this to mean we are not to say God's name in conjunction with any swearing or cursing. However, that is a Greco-Roman, Western-cultural understanding of "name" and not an Eastern Hebraic one. That cultural context matters because Moses and the people of the exile were not Greek or Roman. They were Hebrew and very much Eastern in their philosophy and manner of thinking. Therefore, to understand the passage, we must understand what a name was to them. *Shem Yahweh* means "the name of Yahweh," but the name is not something uttered. It translates more closely as the character of God.

Furthermore, this is why being a slave to God was better than being a slave to Egypt. The people did not know this at the time and were long to convince. Benner's *Ancient Hebrew Lexicon* defines the word as "The wind, or breath, of someone or something is its character."[1]

This understanding makes sense when you think of the last time you spoke with someone after they ate onions and garlic or smoked a cigarette compared to times they had just brushed their teeth or were chewing gum. When we start to understand that the name of God is not the actual "name" but is the character instead, it sheds new light on all the passages that speak of God's name. For example, when Moses said to God, "They are going to ask me 'What's this God's name?' What am I supposed to say to them?" he is not looking for a name but seeking evidence of trustworthy character and believable power. Moses is trying to find something about God into which he can convince the people to put their faith. When we pray in the name of Jesus, there is nothing magical about the letter combinations of the name, but there is power in the character of Jesus because Jesus emptied himself of his ego and filled himself with the character of God. Of course, if you come from a "name it, claim it" background, this is unwelcome news. Nevertheless, for the rest of us, this takes us slightly further under the hood, perhaps giving us some life-changing insights in a new way to look at the "name of God" as we see the rest of the assigned passages deal with being honorable toward not only God but to others as well.

Bringing the Text to Life

A rose by any other name would smell just as sweet, and God, by any other name—Yahweh, El, Elohim, El Shaddai, El Elyon—would still be God. What combination of letters by which we refer to God means very little. How we experience and exhibit the character of God is what matters. Even more important is that this is key in our call to become like Jesus, who extended an invitation to the relationship shared by God and Son (John 14:20; 17:22-23). Jesus challenges us to do more than call him Lord. He challenges us to take on his character, as he took on the character of God (Luke 6:46). It is not enough to call ourselves Christians if we do not intend to move forward by loving others, which breaks the commandment not to take God's character in vain. If we want to avoid this snare, we must learn to love as Jesus loved. Only then will the words of our mouths and the meditations of our hearts be pleasing to God.

October 15, 2023–Twentieth Sunday after Pentecost

Exodus 32:1-14; *Psalm 106:1-6, 19-23; Philippians 4:1-9;*
Matthew 22:1-14

Roland Millington

Preacher to Preacher Prayer

Lord God, open your heart fully to my sisters and brothers as they strive to bring forth your glorification in their sermons.

Commentary

In Exodus 32:1, we begin in a leadership vacuum. Moses is gone, and Aaron is effectively in charge, but as we see, he was not an effective leader, immediately ordered around by the people contrary to God's expectations. God had already given them a complete set of instructions (Exod 20–31), but they now disregard them. Officials rip offerings from unwilling ears (Exod 32:2). The idea of a particular, sacred, and unique Yahwistic worship goes sailing out the window. Their worship resembles the gods of the land surrounding them, the calf being just another adornment. There are no meticulous preparations, but instead a slapdash spectacle ensues, and God, who is personal, active, and all around them, is now seen as a mute, deaf, and blind statue (Exod 32:4-5). Their hearts may have wanted to be close to God, but they picked the 180-degree wrong way to approach it.

Here, Moses is a crucial, go-between figure. "Who will be responsible for the people when the people are irresponsible?"[2] This serves as not only a great question but also a hinge point for these fourteen verses.

The gold brought from Egypt ripped from the ears of the people is then fashioned into a calf. Worthy of note: we spell El *"alef lamed"* in Hebrew. It means "the strong authority." The pictograph for this is *alef*, an ox head representing strength, and a *lamed*, a shepherd's staff.[3] Therefore, Aaron's choice of a bull or a calf to symbolize the god that would lead them to the promised land made sense. It was also regionally familiar.

Aaron's completion of the calf leads to his proclamation of the feast to Yahweh. To the people, they were not abandoning, but honoring God. To God, this was a display of ignorance with a refashioned image suitable only to the people. Their worship, except the play, was reverent worship of Yahweh. Their hearts wanted the right thing. However, the promise of an easy shortcut in Moses's absent leadership proved too much for the people to overcome.

Immediate gratification becomes the rule of the day, and God's slow, steady guidance sloughs off the "stiff-necked people." Notably, "stiff-necked" refers to a stubborn ox that will not turn its neck to point its body in an appropriate direction. They made a god of a golden calf whose neck did not turn, fittingly making a god in their image, a complete reversal of creation in their apostasy. Creation attempts to usurp the creator.

The rest of the chapter is about God and Moses discussing how to deal with their apostasy. God seems interested in abandoning the whole mess, but Moses reminds God to whom these people belong. God reminds Moses that the people first credited Moses with bringing them out of Egypt (Exod 32:1) and then credited the statue (Exod 32:4).

We find an important nuance here. God left the door open for Moses to argue for the people's reprieve from God's wrath. When God said, "leave me alone," it was clear that God was telling Moses what was about to happen and did that for a reason. As much as God guides the people to the promised land, God is guiding Moses to become a more significant leader for this recalcitrant community of former slaves. Moses receives a chance to take his future and run but instead intercedes on behalf of the people. In this way, Moses is exhibiting God's character, or *Shem*, right back to God. That Moses did so to cure a covenantal breach is even more powerfully indicative of that character.

Moses's relationship with God is a close one. More than a supreme commander and general, they appear as intimate friends. Creator and created, yes, but they are closely aligned, and Moses no doubt profoundly experienced God's love. How else would one explain Moses feeling comfortable enough to attempt so boldly to change God's mind?

Moses appeals to reason and glorifies God by stating that God delivered the people, showing his allegiance. He then speaks to God's reputation, explaining that to destroy the people would look bad in the eyes of neighboring nations.

Finally, Moses states his boldest claim. He reminds God of the promise God made. With God's commitment broken, no one would ever follow again. God could easily have told Moses that the people broke the agreement, leaving God free to abandon them. Instead, God took Moses's insight, boldness, and willingness to stand in the gap to heart and honors Moses's pleading.

In this passage, we discover that Moses had his own Jacob moment. He is striving with God, but he is doing it correctly, with tact, candor, reason, and compassion; most important, he is displaying God's character, a sign of maturing faith.

This discourse is a direct contrast to the rebellious striving against God that happened at Massah and Meribah. It would have been foolish for God to dismiss Moses when approaching the subject as God alone would approach it. Throughout the Bible, from Abraham forward, it seems that God likes a good debate, not because

God always wins them, but because people grow in the process of striving appropriately with God.

Bringing the Text to Life

There are some key components in this passage, not the least of which is immediate gratification compared with slow and steady growth. Think fast-food meals versus a feast made at home. Diving into these concepts from the perspective of any of the people in the passages—Moses, Aaron, or the people—should compare them to the perspective of God, as the whole point of this passage is to bring out a challenge to take on God's character.

October 22, 2023–
Twenty-First Sunday after
Pentecost

Exodus 33:12-23 or Psalm 99; Isaiah 45:1-7 or Psalm 96:1-9, (10-13);
1 Thessalonians 1:1-10; Matthew 22:15-22

Dottie Escobedo-Frank

Preacher to Preacher Prayer

God of All, the psalm read on this Twenty-First Pentecost Sunday shows you sitting on the regal spaces of the universe, watching and waiting and calling forth the movements of the earth and sky.

We see your amazing ways, and we marvel. Yet even more, we see that you are a God who loves justice. You understand the boundaries of fairness, and made templates of justice in the heart of Jacob. We can't begin to know how holy you are. Moses, Aaron, and Samuel all cried out to you for help and you answered them. You showed yourself as a forgiving and just God. And today, we too need your help. We need your forgiveness, and your justice. Watch us, and guide us, and renew us, for You alone are holy! Amen.

Commentary

Have you ever asked more from someone you love? Maybe you stated "I need more of your time" or "Could you focus on me as much as you focus on work?" Perhaps you've asked, "From now on, let's eat our meals together without screens" or "Can we do a weekly brunch together?"

I once tried to negotiate the dinner meal as a time when my spouse and I would only speak Spanish, in hopes that our children would learn a new language. Though we discussed it back and forth for some time, I wasn't able to convince my spouse of the benefit of that idea. But other times, when asking for more from someone I love, I have been pleased by the willingness to be heard and seen, and to go deeper in our connection.

Moses seemed to be in a discussion or pleading mode with God. He was asking for God to send someone to help him. God responded that Godself would be with him and help him. Moses must have been delighted! He asked for a friendly helper, and he got God Almighty to walk with him instead. He received more than he asked for, more than he expected.

So, then Moses gives credit to God by saying that only God's presence with them sets them apart from all other people on the earth. However, that wasn't enough for Moses. He was feeling rather bold, so he made another request: "Please show me your glorious presence" (v. 18).

God considered Moses's plea. Knowing what he really wanted was a closeness to God, God made a way. Letting Moses know of the danger of seeing God face-to-face, he instead agreed to show Moses God's back. God points out a gap in a rock where Moses could see without fully experiencing the blinding light of God. God covers Moses's eyes, passes by him, and then removes the hand of God so that Moses can get a glimpse of God's back.

Moses had God going his way! And don't you wish sometimes that your discussions with God could end with God seeing the value of your request, and answering in your favor? Another question to consider: If God told you that God would be present with you through some difficulty, what would be your next request of God? Would you want to see God's face? Would you ask to repair a relationship, or to provide resources, or to mend your broken heart? If you had God going your way after a lengthy argument, what would be your next request?

We are continually pleading our case, or the case of our loved ones, before God. We pray at night and in the morning and we whisper prayers in the daytime, just hoping that God will hear us and do what we ask.

It is good when God goes our way, but sometimes God goes another way, and we don't always get to know why. We can't see the scope of the universe as God does. We don't have the wisdom of eternity as God does. We don't always ask for what God sees that we need: God's presence to be near and constant. Moses requested a deeper connection with God above all else. He wasn't asking God to make him rich, or to fix his family problems, or even to give him the strength of character to lead. He asked for help, and he asked to know God deeper.

What are you asking God for today? Will you be at peace whether God goes your way or you are asked to go God's way? Being faithful can sometimes be a difficulty that requires determination. We don't always get it right, but God sees us, loves us, and desires to lead us.

Bringing the Text to Life

Share a time when you asked God for something and God answered you. Then share a story when you asked God for something and God didn't seem to even hear you; there was silence. Then address the struggle of hearing nothing at times, and of having your prayers answered at other times. Is there a formula for God answering your requests? Can we control God by our prayers? And do we continually make the mistake of trying to control God's outcome for our lives? What do we do with the fact that we cannot predict when God will answer us and when God will be silent? Do our prayers even matter?

Relationship is all about connecting deeper and seeing the other. It is not about demands, but about enlightenment. How do we determine whether our prayer honors the desire of God to be known?

October 29, 2023–
Twenty-Second Sunday after Pentecost

*Deuteronomy 34:1-12 or Psalm 90:1-6, 13-17; Leviticus 19:1-2, 15-18
or Psalm 1; 1 Thessalonians 2:1-8;* **Matthew 22:34-46**

Dottie Escobedo-Frank

Preacher to Preacher Prayer

Creator God, you have been our help in time of need for generations. Even before the mountains were born, or the earth was born, from the forever of the past to the forever of the future, you have shown yourself to be our God. Sometimes you remind us of our humanity: we are mere dust; but a dream. Sometimes you renew us in the morning, reminding us that you are still with us. Come to us, O God! Come quickly and bring your compassion and mercy. Fill us every morning so that we can celebrate who you are. For though we have suffered for our troubles, your kindness covered us with mercy. May the work we do last forever. Amen.

Commentary

Math is not my forte. But after taking some basic classes in high school and college, and learning the theoretical basics of statistics in my master's programs, I figured out something very simple: math boils down to basic addition, subtraction, multiplication, and division. If you understand the basics, the more difficult concepts of geometry, algebra, and so on can be understood. Statistics is based on learning how numbers can be presented as true value or manipulated unfairly. Beware of statistical analysis and make sure the data presented represent the whole picture.

In Hebrew history, there were 613 laws or commandments to be followed. What a weight! One had to know all the laws, and then follow all of them! David reduced these to 11 essential rules (Ps 15). Micah limited them to 3 (Mic 6:8). And then Jesus came along and reduced all 613 commands to 2: "You must love the Lord your God with all your heart, with all your being, and with all your mind. This is the first and greatest commandment. And the second is like it: You must love your neighbor as you love yourself. All the Law and the Prophets depend on these two commands" (Matt 22:37-40).

In the complexities of life, sometimes simplifying things brings about the greatest clarity. Jesus was put to the test to see if he would choose one command over the other. However, Jesus was good at discerning others and answering hard questions with simple truths. He didn't let the confusion of others cloud his clear and certain understanding of the kingdom of God. Jesus called for a new way to live with simple rules that pierced through the complications of life. And so Jesus said, "Love God with everything that is in you (heart, being, mind) and love your neighbor as much as you love yourself. That's all that matters." Simple is better. Simple is understandable. Simple is doable.

The simple movement that has swept our consumeristic world has the same basic premise: less is more. This movement understands that the more items we own, the more time is lost in caring for those items or in getting new ones. The number of people who have chosen to live simply, without the overabundance of things, has grown steadily in the past decade. Society has experienced the burden of the stuff of life, and many have chosen to set themselves free from the responsibility of ownership in favor of the freedom of living light. The simple movement has added value to a peaceful life.

Jesus, knowing that we needed to keep religion and rules simple, named only two things that matter: loving God and loving neighbor. That's it. For every decision we have to make, we can ask ourselves only two questions: Does this show my love for God? Does this action show love for my neighbor? That's it.

Bringing the Text to Life

Simplification means letting go of the things that hold us back. Every process of simplifying means releasing and letting go. Just as the Hebrews had to release all the laws that constrained their hearts and lives, we too have to let go of the rules and rituals that no longer feed us or bring us peace. God might just have a new way of drawing us close to God and to our neighbor, but we need to be open to the new and simple forms of relationship.

Check out *Minimalism*, a documentary featuring the story of Joshua Fields Millburn and Ryan Nicodemus. These two young, successful businessmen walked away from high-paying jobs to find peace in simplicity. And they have sparked a movement across the globe by their story.

Read *The Life-Changing Magic of Tidying Up: The Japanese Art of Decluttering and Organizing* by Marie Kondo. This best-selling book provides advice on how to release the stuff that clutters our homes, and then explains ways to keep things in order through the details of homemaking. The author even gives suggestions on how to best fold your socks and T-shirts for a more perfect image of order.

Perhaps the cluttered form of our religion is holding us back from the simple faith that Jesus taught us. Cluttered faith can come at the cost of loving God freely and caring for neighbors extravagantly. When too much is required of us, we drown in the details and lose the simple message of love.

November 1, 2023– All Saints Day

Revelation 7:9-17 or Psalm 34:1-10, 22; 1 John 3:1-3; **Matthew 5:1-12**

Dottie Escobedo-Frank

Preacher to Preacher Prayer

God of all creation, we will sing your praises forever. Even when we suffer, we listen for the joy. You have given us reason to be grateful and happy! We have sought you in the middle of our fears, and you have taken away our shame. When we were in the hell of suffering, you heard us and saved us! From every side, you protect and deliver us, so we understand that need to "taste and see that the LORD is good" (Ps 34:8 NRSV). We know our happiness comes from taking refuge in you. Amen.

Commentary

On All Saints Day, we remember those special people in our lives who have passed on to eternity. The honoring and remembering on this day every year is a way to bring back the influential and loving people who knew us well, shaped us, and loved us deeply.

When I think of the saints who have gone before me, I remember my grandmother Gertrude Roberts, who loved to watch *General Hospital*. She would explain all the characters to me and talk about them as if they were real. I would come and join her as often as I could, just so I could hear her tell their stories. Grandma sent me plane tickets when I was homesick in college. She laughed and cried every time we said hello and goodbye, because she knew that every visit might be the last one. My fondest image is when I would go to her house unexpectedly and see her sitting in her comfy chair reading her Bible by the light of the lamp. She loved God. And she loved me.

My father was also a special saint to me. He always provided inspiration and wider vision, and listened to every soul that came his way. He was a saint while he was alive, and even more so when he died. I also recall my mother, who would weave stories with such passion and abandon that everyone who heard her would be drawn in. She loved so deeply, studied fervently, wrote passionately, and lived life fully. These are some of the saints whom I remember and bring back to life on this special day.

Special saints in our lives often embody the Beatitudes. As we know, the Beatitudes are sayings that piece together a hard thing with a good thing. They take the hard stuff of life and remind us of the bigger picture and the greater value:

The hopeless are given the kingdom of heaven.
The grieving are made glad.
The humble are provided with a great inheritance.
The ones who hunger and thirst for righteousness, will be made full.
The merciful are given mercy.
The pure in heart get to see God.
The peaceful ones are called God's own children.
The harassed are given the whole kingdom of God, and a reward in heaven.

These words don't make much sense to a logical mind, but to the soul it makes all the sense in the world. My funny grandmother, my saintly father, and my passionate mother were all imperfect, and they all suffered. Yet they found a way to love perfectly and to make sense of an impossible world. They saw beyond the suffering and struggle, and they taught me that God's view is better than any attempt at logic. They taught me how to endure, how to be patient, how to trust, and how to have faith. They helped me grasp the Beatitudes.

You and I will be saints in the Great Beyond someday. What we leave behind to the next generation will be the intangibles and the spiritual understandings of living as a person of faith. Thank God for Grandma, and Dad, and Mom, and all the saints gone before us, who made the Beatitudes a reality.

Bringing the Text to Life

Trying to explain spiritual concepts to people who do not know God is a difficult process. I recall explaining why I give a tithe to the church to a person who never connected with any religion. He argued endlessly that the math didn't add up—that giving away money only left us with less. He couldn't grasp the idea that in giving, we receive.

Abstract spiritual concepts can be difficult to explain and comprehend, which is why it is a challenge for many people to understand the Beatitudes. However, in the depths of our souls, we concur that they are true.

Recall a person in your own life who changed you. What hard things did they teach you (things like the Beatitudes)? What would you have become without their influence? How are you different, better, or challenged because they taught you something that didn't make sense at the time, but you later found to be true? Remember the saints in your own life, and share stories of the ones who were heroes as well as those who taught you by their mistakes.

After you light candles for the persons in your congregation who died in the past year, invite the congregation to light a candle for those saints in their lives. Provide metal containers filled with sand and tea candles. The movement to light their own candles connects the people with their own memories of saints, and provides a way to honor them.

November 5, 2023– Twenty-Third Sunday after Pentecost

Joshua 3:7-17; Psalm 107:1-7, 33-37; Micah 3:5-12; Psalm 43; 1 Thessalonians 2:9-13; Matthew 23:1-12

Cyndi McDonald

Preacher to Preacher Prayer

As once you parted waters and led your people, lead us now. May we look to you about our own way forward. We can only give to others what we have within, and so we pray that your spirit would fill us with your love, joy, and peace. As you have been present and working through generation after generation in the church, be present and at work in our lives today.

Commentary

The texts selected for the first three weeks in November can together form a cohesive series for stewardship or gratitude. The commentaries here are structured to give thanks for the past (November 5), give thanks for the present (November 12), and give thanks for the future (November 19).

In Joshua 3, Moses has passed away and Joshua leads the people. Early in the journey from Egypt, Moses had sent spies into the promised land, and all but Joshua and Caleb reported that the land was filled with giants who could not be conquered. Now, a generation has passed away, and spies report that residents are in fear of the Israelites (Josh 2:24).

Although no pillar of fire or cloud is present, the God who rescued the people from slavery in Egypt and through the parting of the sea is present. Once again waters stand still and the people cross on dry land.

God hasn't changed, but is working in a new way. Rather than one man, Moses, stretching out a shepherd's rod to split the water, this time the waters split when priests carrying the covenant chest stand in the Jordan River. God is at work through people, these priests, and all they carry.

God still works through people and the loads they carry. Although it happens occasionally, most of us did not come to faith by stumbling across a Bible in a hotel room. Rather, it was a person carrying scripture and a love of God in their heart, faithfully teaching a Sunday school class, inviting us to see God at work in new ways. Perhaps it was a friend, carrying a love of God, who inspired a desire to know more about this God.

Do you have a story of a transformative moment in which grace was revealed through the load carried? For myself, it was the volunteer who carried a passion for youth in his heart. As a young adult no longer interested in having the church or God as part of my life, I ran into him in a mall store. He shared that he prayed for me every Friday, and asked if there was any way in particular he could pray for me. He showed a card listing names of former youth, names divided by days of the week. The selfless faithfulness he carried in his heart helped me see God's people in a new way.

The priests who carried the covenant chest were the first to enter the Jordan River. This scripture invites us to give thanks for those who were first: the first to give when someone was in trouble, the first to volunteer in the nursery, the first to forgive and let go of grievances. This, too, is how God works, inspiring us all to give, to serve, to forgive.

Sometimes people don't see themselves as priests or saints. The community in Joshua would have known the priests and their flaws. They would have recognized the priests as people who carried doubts, fears, and hurts. Trust instead that although the crowds following see people with flaws and foibles, it's really God who is leading. The story ends with the priests standing firmly in the river until all Israel, every person in the entire nation, crosses over.

Bringing the Text to Life

As noted above, this can be an opportunity for a three-part stewardship or thanksgiving series, beginning this Sunday by giving thanks for the past. Many churches celebrate All Saints on the following Sunday. If you did not have a November 1 All Saints service, consider sharing stories of the saints within the congregation and the gifts and graces they carried into the chaotic waters of life. If you don't have personal stories about all of the saints being honored, or if there are more saints than time available, tell a few stories without using the names. You'll find that more than one saint made a neighbor welcome, more than one saint cut grass for a neighbor in the hospital, more than one saint made the visitor feel like they were the one blessed when they came to offer comfort in the hospital. In a smaller church, with fewer saints named, you can share again the stories of treasured saints rather than limiting your examples to those who have joined the church triumphant in the last year.

A children's sermon could allude to the following chapter, Joshua 4, which is not in the lectionary for this date. Joshua has the people set up stones as a reminder of how God helped the people through the water. Set river stones in the room for children to find, each in a place that serves as a reminder of how God has been present for us. A stone could be on the baptismal font. Every time we enter the sanctuary and see the font we are reminded that we belong to God. A stone on the Communion Table teaches that every time we see the Communion Table we remember Jesus's meal and the covenant he gives. A stone on the window sill next to a stained glass window signifies that when we see the window we remember the scene depicted. If there is a name listed there, we remember that person and how God was working through them. For those whose worship is primarily done over video, expand the locations beyond the sanctuary.

November 12, 2023– Twenty-Fourth Sunday after Pentecost

Joshua 24:1-3a, 14-25; *Psalm 78:1-7; 1 Thessalonians 4:13-18;*
Matthew 25:1-13

Cyndi McDonald

Preacher to Preacher Prayer

God of the ages, giver of all that is good, open our eyes to the blessings that surround us. Help us to be thankful for today. Amen.

Commentary

The texts selected for the first three weeks in November can form a cohesive series for stewardship or gratitude. Today's scripture encourages us to give thanks for how God is present, and is sandwiched between themes of giving thanks for the past (November 5) and giving thanks for the future (November 19).

At the end of his life, Joshua gathers the tribes of Israel around him. He reminds them of their history, beginning with Terah, the father of Abraham, through the time in Egypt and in the wilderness. God has been with them in every age.

Joshua reminds them of the ways they have been richly blessed. They live in cities they did not build. Although they did not plant these, they harvest from rich vineyards and olive groves. Now they have a choice. Who will they serve? Will they serve the Lord or will they serve the gods of the lands that surround them?

Although the examples Joshua gives seem archaic, the questions he presents are ones for every generation. Will you recognize your blessings as being from God? Will you be content to think and live according to the culture of your day, or will you recognize these as idols and instead serve the Lord?

For example, the graduate may think of a degree with pride, and see this as something for which she worked. But look further for the grace. The student was able to read textbooks because of parents who read to her when she was a toddler and encouraged a love of reading. Teachers provided the grounding necessary for succeeding academically. Parents helped with tuition or the car and gas to get to summer jobs. A student's tuition covers only a fraction of an institution's expenses. Taxes and charitable donations cover much of this.

We live on roads we did not pave. We grow up in homes we did not build. We sit on pews that others purchased and in sanctuaries that others built. How might we recognize grace in our lives?

Joshua's recount of their blessings also reminds them that they get to choose, rather than let the surrounding culture determine their course. Likewise, we too can choose to be content, in any and every situation (Phil 4:12), rather than allow a consumerist culture to drive our desires. When a friend has a new car, will you be happy for them, or wish for a newer model for yourself? Will you unthinkingly long for what others have, envying vacations and well-behaved children pictured on social-media feeds? Or will we choose to see all we have as gift and grace. Will we value people and relationships? Will we choose to be thankful? To find joy in serving God? To look away from consumption and toward acquiring fruits of the spirit like peace, patience, and kindness?

Bringing the Text to Life

Suggest scenarios in which the natural response is frustration or complaint. Instead of the idols suggested by consumerist culture—the perfect job, the perfect family, the perfect home—how can we instead recognize in each setting the ways God has given and blessed us? Ask rhetorically, providing your own answers, or be brave and encourage the congregation to call out their own ideas, and in this way strengthen their own gratitude muscles. They may identify blessings beyond your own! The following scenarios could be adapted for your context:

1. Thanksgiving is next week. A relative calls at the last minute and is arriving on a flight at 6 A.M. Instead of getting a good night's sleep, you are setting the alarm to get up at 4 A.M. for the drive to the airport. (Potential blessings: You have relatives. You have a good relationship and they want to be together for the holiday. You have a car. You can drive. You are able to take time off from work to get them.)

2. You are in the grocery store with your children. You thought you were done, but the older child is saying, "Mom, Mom, I just remembered that we have a science project due tomorrow. We need to get a poster board for my science project. I might need some vinegar and baking soda. I might need lots of red food coloring." All the while the younger child is interrupting with, "Mom, can I have a pack of Skittles? Could I get some Lunchables to take to school? Why do we always get my brother's favorite cereal? Why can't I pick out the cereal?" (Blessings: You have children who are healthy. We have a school system where children can get an education and a teacher who cares enough to suggest projects rather than simply lecture. You have enough funds to pay for groceries.)

3. You are late for work and traffic comes to a halt. You sit on the expressway with what seems like thousands of cars, and even though you know it won't help, you want to press on the horn. You hear sirens and see multiple ambulances and police cars approaching. This is going to take a while to clear. Your boss will be furious about the delay. (Blessings: You have a job. You have a car. There are ambulances and police to assist people in accidents. God has called people to serve in the health care system and as police officers.)

November 19, 2023– Twenty-Fifth Sunday after Pentecost

Judges 4:1-7; Psalm 123; Zephaniah 1:7, 12-18;
Psalm 90:1-8, (9-11), 12; *1 Thessalonians 5:1-11; Matthew 25:14-30*

Cyndi McDonald

Preacher to Preacher Prayer

Teach us to number our days, not from sunrise to sunset, but in lives changed.

Commentary

This is the third in a potential November series for stewardship or gratitude, in which the congregation is urged to give thanks for the past and present (November 5 and 12) with a third Sunday giving thanks for the future. A stewardship series could include a time to give thanks for the future by making a commitment to support God's work through the church.

The psalm gives thanks for the past and present. The Lord has been our help from generation to generation, and in eternity past God is God! Although the lectionary selection describes our short lives as hard work and trouble (v. 10), later verses speak of God renewing the soul so that each day we rejoice and celebrate (vv. 14 and 15). There are reasons to give thanks each day.

Perhaps that is the psalmist's intent. If we but recognized the brevity of our days, we would treat each day as precious. Days would be lived fully, joyfully serving God rather than filled with dread and paralyzed with fear. The concluding verse in the lectionary selection, "teach us to number our days so we can have a wise heart" (v. 12) suggests that if we truly measured our life, we would live these days differently.

This is more than just the ordinary advice to make the most of a finite life. Isaiah 40:8 speaks similarly of grass that dries up and flowers that wither, yet accompanies these with the reminder that our God's word will exist forever. The psalmist similarly suggests that God looks back on a thousand years much like a human thinks back on yesterday. We are more than our short lives when we connect with an eternal God.

A physical structure may stand for centuries. An institution may last for generations. But a life changed is eternal.

I learned this in an unexpected way, serving in a church as the finance committee chair. After her passing, the family of Dottie Smith (name changed) gave a large gift for youth mission in her honor. Dottie was a champion of the youth mission trips, hammering on roofs with them in her younger years, packing sandwiches and cooking suppers in her elder years.

When I met with the family, I explained that the funds were carefully invested in certificates of deposits—very safe investments with little risk—and I had worked with parents to craft a policy that would finance youth mission trips for decades, perhaps even indefinitely. We would only use the interest from the fund to pay for scholarships. Youth participating in the trip would have to raise funds and match the contributions from the fund—this would ensure that only motivated youth, who wanted to participate in these trips as mission trips (not just fun trips), would be helped by the fund.

But instead of commendation for the care with which the youth leaders and I had administrated the fund, the family responded with silence. Finally, Dottie's daughter spoke up. "We didn't want you to invest the money in CDs. We wanted you to invest the money in youth. We don't care if the money lasts—in fact, we'd like it if the money was spent soon. We want you to invest this money in youth, not in some bank account."

I wanted to invest prudently so that funds would last beyond my own short span. But maybe Dottie bringing along her sons and daughters on these mission trips had helped them to see what I had not seen. They had seen the lives of youth changed eternally—even those youth who don't really want to be there but seemed to tag along for the ride.

Compare the life spans to life impact. A table in the fellowship hall lasts a decade or three, until you consider the impact of spiritual friendships formed as people sit around these for meals. A light bulb in a Sunday school classroom may seem like it has a short lifespan, until you hear stories of lives changed and connecting with the eternal during this time in Sunday school.

Bringing the Text to Life

In his humorous TED Talk, "Inside the Mind of a Master Procrastinator," Tim Urban describes how deadlines impact the likelihood of completing goals.[1] Unfortunately, the most important goals (a healthy prayer life, good relationships, regular exercise) don't come with a deadline. He depicts a life calendar, with one box per week in a ninety-year life. It is smaller than expected, a remarkable visual of how few "boxes" remain even in a long life.

In the movie *Big Fish*, Edward and his friends dare one another to visit the swamp witch. They have heard that to look into her glass eye is to see your own eventual death. Unlike the others who are fearful, Edward argues that knowing your end helps you live: "If dying was all you thought about, it could kind of screw you up. But it could kind of help you, couldn't it? Because you'd know that everything else you can survive."[2]

For the blessing of commitments, let the congregation know you are reading further, to the last verse of the psalm: "Let the kindness of the Lord our God be over us. Make the work of our hands last. Make the work of our hands last!" (v. 17).

November 23, 2023– Thanksgiving Day

Deuteronomy 8:7-18; Psalm 65; 2 Corinthians 9:6-15; Luke 17:11-19

Paul Cho

Preacher to Preacher Prayer

Gracious God, you give yourself to us so freely, so openly. We pray that we would not just receive your great gift to us in Jesus Christ, but that we would also give of ourselves to your creation and all who inhabit it, freely, openly, and with great thanksgiving. Amen.

Commentary

While thanksgiving in and of itself is an appropriate and arguably necessary response as a faithful Christian, I also feel a certain uneasiness when reading scripture of God's promise to the people of Israel of land, water, and the prosperity that will come from it. On the one hand, I feel gratitude and peace in knowing that God is leading us to a good land, like the good shepherd leading his flock to green pastures and still waters. On the other, I feel anguish thinking about the inhabitants who will soon be displaced. I feel caught somewhere in between.

Perhaps, more than the text itself, I am grieved by how scriptures like our text from Deuteronomy have been used to amplify or even justify our imperial/colonial ways to conquer others. It is as if the text provides convincing evidence that a group of people uniquely bound together are more superior than another. Not only so, it also says indirectly that stronger beings taking from the weaker ones are a part of the natural order or God-willed. What a terrible thought to behold and yet, how often have we resorted to similar ideologies.

I was born in Korea at a time when victims of imperialism were still around. I grew up in America bullied because of my slanted eyes and larger head-to-body ratio. I cannot help thinking of those who live in the aftermath of domineering power. How did they give thanks when everything had been taken from them? How does one give thanks to their oppressor's God? It is not difficult to understand why so few Native Americans submit to a Eurocentric Christ. There needs to be a different way to frame our faith. We need to consider context.

Whether you are considering the passage from Deuteronomy or the theme of Thanksgiving Day, context matters, and context is powerful.

I do not doubt that the Pilgrims were in good faith, thanking God. They did not come to this new land seeking to harm those who were already here. No one at the original Thanksgiving table could have known what history would later tell us, about how the arrival of Pilgrims led to the decimation of Native Americans.

Furthermore, the first Pilgrims settled the land with 102 people but they lost 45 that winter of 1620–21, leaving their population nearly halved. Despite popular images of a full Thanksgiving feast table signifying a bountiful harvest, that first year was tremendously difficult. They were barely getting by. This day of thanksgiving was not happenstance. Thanksgiving was a deliberate act of faith. Their thanksgiving was rooted in the trust that God was with them.

The context for our reading in Deuteronomy is also significant. Moses gave these instructions to the Israelites at a critical moment in their history. They would need to reconsider how God is present in their lives. Instead of receiving and collecting manna each morning, they would need to go out to find fruits, and sow seeds to reap crops. Instead of striking a stone for water, they would need to dig wells and retrieve water from established sources. Instead of relying on the constant protection of cloud cover by day and a pillar of fire by night, they would need to build up their own shelters with stones and metals gathered up from hours and hours of digging and forging. God would be present with them—in the waters that shower the crops and keep the streams flowing, and in the rays of sun that nourish the plants and give them warmth. Yet, God's presence would be different. It may be that because God was present in different ways, they would fail to remember God was there with them all along. So, Moses instructs them to give thanks to God, deliberately, especially when they are found prosperous, for God was with them and enabled them.

On the one hand, you have the Israelites, promised with new land in which they will prosper, instructed to give thanks. On the other hand, you have the Pilgrims just hanging on to their lives in this foreign land with their new neighbors, giving thanks.

While I imagine that the pilgrims were reading this text in Deuteronomy and hoping that the same promise would be fulfilled in their lives, for both the Israelites or the Pilgrims, thanksgiving was not merely bound to a bountiful harvest, or prosperity for that matter. And neither should our thanksgiving be dependent on what we have. Rather, let us consider our personal context and offer our authentic thanksgiving.

Bringing the Text to Life

My mind can hardly comprehend the complexities of how God works in our midst. At the transplant wing of a hospital where I once served as a chaplain stood a mother praying desperately for her son's recovery. His only chance was through a successful liver transplant. She shared with me how wrong it felt initially to pray for a donor knowing full well that it would mean a loss of a loved one for another family. But she was also grateful in some sense because the health crisis had brought the two of them closer. Frankly, I was a bit lost for words myself. Her son is in a health crisis, but there is also thanksgiving for the reconciled relationship. Then there was hope for recovery but only through a donor. I wasn't sure how I would pray so I asked her to pray and that I would join with her. Through prayer, she helped me to see past my dilemma. In no way was she praying for some healthy soul to suddenly pass away so that their organs might provide life for her son. Rather, she was filled with deep compassion for the family who would ultimately be facing loss, and the following decision to go through with the organ donation. If anything, she was praying moreso for them than her son at the moment. She expressed deep thanksgiving.

One morning several months later, I was called in to visit a family who had lost a loved one overnight in the ER after a bicycle accident. I expected to meet a distraught family but was met with a father and his younger daughter who were somewhat composed. After our formalities, he began to weep tears I will never fully know. He then told me that he was "going to do it." "What is it that you're going to do?" I asked. He was going to donate his son's organs. His son had always been so loving, always had a radiating smile, was always looking to help others. "My son would want it." His daughter, not having said a single word, sobbing onto her dad's arms, shook her head in agreement. So, I prayed with them as best I could, with thanksgiving.

My mind cannot make sense of how people process pain, suffering, and loss. Yet, over and over again, I have found faithful Christians who are able to give thanks, despite their situation, because of how God is present with them. May we find God in our midst and offer our authentic thanksgiving.

November 26, 2023– Reign of Christ–Twenty-Sixth Sunday after Pentecost

Ezekiel 34:11-16, 20-24; Psalm 100; Ezekiel 34:11-16, 20-24; Psalm 95:1-7a; Ephesians 1:15-23; **Matthew 25:31-46**

Paul Cho

Preacher to Preacher Prayer

Oh God, my God, you are my great liberator. Set me free to see where I do not, to love in the ways you've taught, and proclaim that your mercies fail not. Let me breathe in the Spirit that gives me life, and be strengthened from within to shine Christ's light. Amen.

Commentary

Thinking upon Jesus as one who separates people is rather difficult to imagine, considering just how inclusive Christ had been in his ministry. Beyond gathering up the disciples who themselves were quite diverse, I think of the Samaritan woman at the well, the Syro-Phoenician woman who sought healing for her daughter, and the centurion and his servant. Jesus was inclusive of people's gender, socioeconomic status, and their origins. In a way, Jesus was the great unifier of people and is still the reason why we, the church universal, seek to be fully inclusive.

However, this story of Jesus separating the sheep from goats and sending the goats away is different from the radically welcoming Christ I have grown so fond of. It seems antithetical to Christ's boundless love. At the same time, as one who also wrestles in the margins, I do sense a kind of peace that comes with finality at the time of Christ's reign. While I am grateful for Christ's radical welcome, I have also grieved how the church has endured injustice within our sacred community. We have used Christ's inclusive nature as the anchor to allow injustice to prevail, a rhetoric often given by those in power to allow those who abuse to keep abusing. It is painful to endure and painful to imagine this vicious system continuing indefinitely.

My peace and thanksgiving come from knowing that at the time of Christ's full reign, injustice will be uprooted and systems of oppression will be brought down once and for all. If that future of liberty and justice requires the separation of sheep from goats, then so be it. In fact, I am grateful for it.

This, of course, increases the importance of where we will be standing in the mix at that unknown yet certain future. Thankfully, Jesus tells us the traits we should have as sheep of his flock. We should consider those who are hungry, thirsty, naked, sick, imprisoned, and the stranger, and be moved to serve them, "the least of these." I am sure that you already do.

I am not an expert but from what I gather, the difference between sheep and goats, among many, is goats are self-sufficient. Goats, especially feral goats that have escaped into the wild, will survive at a higher rate than feral sheep. Unlike wild sheep, the coat of feral sheep, which were bred for their wool, makes them quite vulnerable. Perhaps what distinguishes the sheep from the goats is our spiritual position of relying on Christ as opposed to relying on our own industry. This is not to say we should not be industrious, but rather, that we remain on the working front and remain open to be led by the movement of the Holy Spirit. How are we in the spiritual practice of depending on Christ to serve "the least of these"? Could it be that we have become disengaged in our service and no longer seek Christ's guidance? Have we become self-sufficient and grown content in thinking that we are doing enough?

John 12:8 tells us that the poor will always be among us. Therefore, by extension, we must always be in the work of ministering and providing for the poor, "the least of these," in spirit and in body. Should we ever be in a position where "the least of these" are not in our midst, let us look with critical eyes to the ways we have become self-sufficient and content. The work for justice is and always will be in need until Christ's full reign.

Bringing the Text to Life

The Inn of Southern Arizona was birthed near the time of the celebration of Christ's birth in 2016. Asylum-seeking families in the midst of legal proceedings were granted legal status to be in the United States. They were dropped off at transit stations where they waited for their contact within the US to purchase tickets for them. Spending a single night at a station would be a rough day for us. For these families, it could take several days. Mind you, they hardly had anything on them. Even the laces of their shoes were removed when they were held for processing. They had no food, no water, no money, just the clothes on their backs. It would be winter time and many of them would be scheduled to travel to places like New Jersey, Ohio, and Washington, DC, wearing just a T-shirt, pants, and sandals.

The United Methodist churches in the Desert Southwest Conference joined together with the United Methodist Committee on Relief to set up a temporary shelter for these traveling families, and the Inn of Southern Arizona was born. Thousands of people from all over the world were sheltered there before their first anniversary, and over ten thousand individuals by their second. Their work continues even to the time of this writing, the second year into the COVID-19 pandemic. Although their personhood was not in any way poor, their circumstances sure made them "the least of these."

Your annual conference likely has its own ministries serving the "least of these" in your communities. Your church may even have outreach programs. Yet, how often do we turn our attention away because we think that we or the church have done enough? In what ways have we become like goats, self-sufficient and content with our support? Examining the "least of these" in our midst with a self-critical eye, and working toward eradicating injustice needs to continue. Let us be on the side that will celebrate the end of injustice at the time of Christ's reign.

December 3, 2023–First Sunday of Advent

*Isaiah **64:1-9**; Psalm 80:1-7, 17-19; 1 Corinthians 1:3-9; Mark 13:24-37*

David K. Johnson

Preacher to Preacher Prayer

Loving God, we know waiting can be challenging. We also know you are faithful. In the moments when life is hard, help us to remember you are there for us. May we be able to sit at the place of waiting and preparation. We are on the edge of a grand celebration. Amen.

Commentary

When I think of the Christmas season, my mind goes to hope, love, joy, and peace. I enjoy the celebration. However, the holiday season is not always full of cheer for everyone. This may be why the first Sunday of Advent has the option for a scripture of lament. This week's text is not personal but a communal lament for the postexilic Jerusalem. God's chosen people did not feel like a chosen people because they returned to their homeland in ruins after seventy years in captivity.

When you come home, there is a desire to return to what was, but this was not possible for God's people. Everything the people held dear was gone, including the temple. The temple was the center of life, and now it was rubble. This was not the life anyone pictured when they thought of going home.

When I was growing up, we never stayed in one house for very long. My parents would purchase a house, remodel it, then sell it. I was always jealous of my friends who could go back to their childhood homes and rooms. When I would go back to their homes in college, their living rooms and bedrooms would be just how I remembered them from high school, which brought me comfort. This was not the experience for the Israelites. Their experience was like being part of a bad dream, and they yearned for God to come and set things right.

The people lived in a unique space of knowing God's faithfulness and also feeling God's absence. In the first part of the pericope, you can hear the brokenness in their voices as they exclaim, "If only you would tear open the heavens and come down!" (Isa 64:1). How many of your congregants are in a similar place? They believe in

God's faithfulness but wonder why God is not showing up and making their lives better? These feelings are both contemporary and ancient. They are points of connection throughout time for the followers of God.

As scripture points out, even though they were God's chosen people, the Israelites still went through tragedy. Some felt their actions led to difficulty. "But you were angry when we sinned; you hid yourself when we did wrong" (Isa 64:5). There was a feeling of guilt for past wrongs and, at the same time, understanding that God was still working. There is authenticity in this pericope; God's people are trying to understand the tension of these two truths: they were God's people and their lives were not going well.

Advent is a challenging journey of tension between the troubles around us and the promises of God's beautiful future. Perhaps one of the gifts the pastor can give the congregation during Advent is acknowledging there will be trouble in this world, that the tension we feel when we trust in God's faithfulness and seem to miss God's presence links us with the experiences of the earliest people. And the exclamation "If only you would tear open the heavens and come down!" is not only their cry, but ours as well—a cry that God answers with the gift of his Son, if only we will wait for his arrival.

There is a desire to quickly get to Christmas and forget Advent. It is human to want to get to the celebration and skip over the preparation and the period of waiting. But Advent allows us to sit in the tension and the brokenness of our reality. During this season, we, as God's people, are preparing ourselves for a celebration. We are preparing for the promises of God's beautiful future, when God will come down.

Bringing the Text to Life

Christopher Davis, a pastor and associate dean at Memphis Theological Seminary, tells the story of when he and his oldest son when to Toys "R" Us.[1] After they arrived, Christopher turned around and could not find his son. The parent panic overcame him, and he began to frantically search for him, but to no avail. In his search, Christopher found a security guard who offered to help find his son.

Christopher asked if he could look at the store's surveillance system. As the guard and Christopher scanned the store through the camera system, they found his son! The guard allowed Christopher to use the intercom system to speak to his son. Christopher called his son by name and then said, "Stay where you are; I am coming."

How many of your people need to hear those words? God is coming to find you while you are feeling lost and abandoned. No matter what tension is in your life, God is faithful and God is coming. Our faith points to God who will tear open the heavens, a God who will come down and let us live in grand expectation. God's love for us is so extravagant that he sent his son. The wait was worth it because Christ is coming for us. The birth of Christ is a celebration that is worth all of the tension and preparation, because God heard our cries and came down.

December 10, 2023–Second Sunday of Advent

Isaiah 40:1-11; Psalm 85:1-2, 8-13; 2 Peter 3:8-15a; Mark 1:1-8

David K. Johnson

Preacher to Preacher Prayer

Ever-present God, when we are busy running around for Advent, remind us to slow down. Slow us down and remind us you are with us, and we have the honor of preaching your good news. Amen.

Commentary

When I was growing up, one of my favorite Christmas traditions was the lighting of the Advent candles. Reading the liturgy and seeing the glow of the candles was awe-inspiring. It always felt like an honor when the pastor asked our family to be part of the service to light one of the candles. Another cherished tradition was going over to my grandparents for breakfast on Christmas morning. All the family would gather to exchange gifts, eat, and enjoy one another's company. After my grandparents passed away, we no longer gathered at my dad's childhood home with the extended family. I was in seminary during this season, and Christmas did not feel like Christmas. Finding comfort when life changes is hard. It can be painful when old traditions become impossible to continue because you can no longer go back to places that were once holy ground.

Isaiah 39 ends with statements like "Days are coming when all that is in your house, which your ancestors have stored up until this day, will be carried to Babylon. Nothing will be left, says the Lord" (v. 6). While chapter 39 ends on a grim note from the tragedy of the seventy-year Babylonian exile, chapter 40 makes a shift by beginning with "Comfort, comfort my people! says your God" (v. 1). In exile, Israel had lamented repeatedly, and there was no comfort or comforter, but now God had come to comfort the oppressed and suffering. God proclaimed Israel would become a great nation. Through God, Israel had defeated enemies and was freed from slavery.

However, when the Babylonians triumphed, it seemed God was absent. Had God abandoned them when they needed God the most? Eventually, the Israelites were able to return to their homeland, but their home no longer brought comfort due to the destruction caused by the Babylonians. People often return to their old patterns and behaviors because there is comfort in old ways. But the temple was destroyed; going back to the old ways was not an option. The old habits and rhythms of life, which once brought comfort, no longer seemed like an option. Change is often complex and finding comfort in the new can be challenging. God's people needed something to hold on to and help them move forward.

Some scholars believe there is more than one writer for this book due to the drastic shift from the words of brokenness to a healing song. Even when speaking about comfort, there is still an acknowledgment of their sinful past, "Speak compassionately to Jerusalem, and proclaim to her that her compulsory service has ended, that her penalty has been paid, that she has received from the Lord's hand double for all her sins!" (v. 2). This comfort comes because their service has been fulfilled, and the Israelites' sins had been forgiven. It can be disorienting when people come out of a season of sin and brokenness. There may be a feeling of distrust or that any kindness is undeserved. God has matched their sin with a double portion of grace because God's intention was redemption and not destruction. Healing and holiness were the telos of the relationship between God and God's people.

Bringing the Text to Life

During the season of 2020, I yearned for the predictable and familiar. In 2020, *The Office* was the most streamed TV show with over 57 billion minutes watched.[2] My binge-watching added to those numbers because watching a comedy show where I knew the characters and what would happen next brought me comfort. There would not be any surprises for me as I watched life unfold in Scranton, Pennsylvania, and I liked that. In reality, life around me was changing too rapidly, so I found peace in the familiar. Something is comforting about the familiar. It might not be a television show, but it could be food, music, books, or even habits. When there is a lot of change around us, people find comfort in what they know. The known is safe and has a low level of risk. How many of your church members yearn for the security of the familiar?

Staying in the familiar and comfortable is sometimes necessary and needed. The Israelites had been through generational trauma. They required some healing, which reconnected them to the God who loved them and was there for them. "Raise it; don't be afraid; say to the cities of Judah, 'Here is your God!'" (v. 9). The people of God needed a reminder of God's presence in their lives. They also needed a reminder that the things of the world are temporary and God is eternal: "The grass dries up; the flower withers, but our God's word will exist forever" (v. 8). This scripture is a reminder of the steadfastness of God. Even if their temple and old ways were gone, God remained.

Comfort was coming; God was bringing comfort through Jesus. This is the anticipation and expectation of Advent. Even if our Advent traditions never return to pre-pandemic precedents, even if our Christmas Eve services never look and feel the way they once did, our comfort is not found in the flickering light of candles or the sound of "Silent Night" filling a sanctuary; our comfort is found in Christ the Messiah.

December 17, 2023–Third Sunday of Advent

Isaiah 61:1-4, 8-11; Psalm 126; **1 Thessalonians 5:16-24**; *John 1:6-8, 19-28*

David K. Johnson

Preacher to Preacher Prayer

God, we are grateful for this joyful season as we prepare for the birth of Jesus. Help us to slow enough to remember who you are in our lives and be thankful. We pray Advent is a season where we can be more like Christ each day.

Commentary

As a pastor, I have a confession. I love some of the shallow parts of Christmas. From the ugly Christmas sweaters to the obnoxious decorations, I love them. When the church changes from green to purple, I get excited. This means I can finally decorate my office and start wearing my tacky Christmas garb. It brings great joy to my life. For me, it is the most wonderful time of the year. But is Christmas the only season of life where we are called to be joyful? I think Paul in 1 Thessalonians would disagree.

First Thessalonians 5:16-18 says, "Rejoice always. Pray continually. Give thanks in every situation because this is God's will for you in Christ Jesus." "Rejoice" here is not used as a suggestion but as a command. As followers of Christ, we are called to be joyful as an act of obedience. Jesus said, "I have said these things to you so that my joy will be in you and your joy will be complete" (John 15:11). Joy is not just a feeling when everything is going well, but it is also a way of life that comes from a deliberate act of our will. It is not solely passive but also an active way we choose to live. Paul is calling us to see the joy of God's creation everywhere we go, so we can become people of celebration and joy. This is not a call to a sugar-coated or false view of life; there are seasons of lament and brokenness. However, if joy is our primary posture, it changes how we live out our lives in the world.

Paul then implores us to "pray continually." Prayer is our way to commune with God. This is not an invitation to a monastic way of life, but it is how we remember who God is in our life. Throughout scripture, we see people forget who God is in their lives. It is difficult to forget someone if you are in constant communication with them. Taking time to pray allows us to slow down to hear the voice of God, allowing a deeper intimacy with the one who loves us. Remembering God changes how you see yourself and the world around you.

"Give thanks in every situation." During the holiday season, there are many ways and reasons to be thankful. Most of the people around us tend to be in good spirits, good food abounds, and most important, we get to celebrate the birth of Christ! It is important to note that Paul is saying to give thanks in every situation and not about every situation. Everything does not happen for a reason or is God's will. Things happen every day that are not the will of God. Even if life is going wrong, we can choose to give thanks to God for the good gifts in our lives. For instance, we all know pastoring is tough; I keep notes of thanks from parishioners to remind me of my call and that sometimes I get it right. Those letters keep me thankful.

God is inviting us to the gift of having a life of joy, prayer, and thankfulness; "this is God's will" for us. As people of faith, we want to live in the will of God. God's will allows us to live a more beautiful and holy life. It seems countercultural to decide to live a life of joy, to slow down enough to have meaningful conversations, and give thanks. Yet, this is the culture God wants us to nurture. How would your life or the life of your people change if you lived the disciplined life of joy, prayer, and thanks?

Bringing the Text to Life

Have you ever had to set anything back to factory settings? Perhaps your computer or phone has been on the fritz, and you tried everything you could to fix it, but your last resort was to set it to the factory settings. Then by some miracle, all the bugs were gone, and the device starts working well. What if Advent was the season to factory reset—to reset from living a life of anxiety, dread, and hurry? New seasons bring about a unique opportunity. Instead of waiting until the new year for resolutions, Advent brings about the gift of seeing and living in new ways. It invites us into a season of joy.

One of my favorite lines from the movie *Elf* is, "The best way to spread Christmas cheer is singing loud for all to hear."[3] Buddy the Elf is the epitome of Christmas joy and helps everyone he encounters live into that joy. We do not all have Buddy's level of over-the-top joy, but maybe we too can spread joy with everyone.

Advent is a time of preparation that can be challenging, especially as the season's busyness intensifies. Prayer is one way we can prepare our hearts and minds for the coming of Christ and focus on thankfulness. Encouraging your congregation to set a dedicated time each day to pray can give them space to slow down and be with God. Sometimes the only way to slow down and have a conversation with God is to make sure you have it on your calendar.

One of the fan favorites from 2021's *America's Got Talent* was Jane Marczewski, also known as Nightbird. She tweeted, "You can't wait until life isn't hard anymore before you decide to be happy."[4] She won the judges over with a song about her cancer journey. I think Jane took notes from 1 Thessalonians; she is still going through a difficult health journey, yet her default setting is joy, prayer, and thankfulness.

December 24, 2023–Fourth Sunday of Advent

2 Samuel 7:1-11, 16; Psalm 89:1-4, 19-26; Romans 16:25-27;
Luke 1:26-38

Charley Reeb

Preacher to Preacher Prayer

Lord, save us from cynicism and doubt. May the celebration of your birth give birth in us to renewed hope and faith. Like Mary, grant us the courage to believe that you can accomplish what seems impossible to us.

Commentary

What's a preacher to say about this week's gospel text that has not already been said? If you look at past sermons you've preached on this passage you will no doubt find messages on the angel Gabriel's command to Mary not to be afraid (v. 30). You may also find messages about God's unlikely choice of Mary to be the mother of Jesus. God honored her because she was humble of heart and had the courage to believe. Perhaps other sermons took a different approach and reflected on a God who would take notice of someone who seemed so unimportant in the eyes of the world. God takes notice of each of us no matter how insignificant we feel. You may also find sermons that focused on Mary's bold obedience: "I am the Lord's servant. Let it be with me just as you have said" (v. 38). We need more obedient people like Mary who boldly trust God. All of these messages are worthy to be preached again. Maybe one of these ideas just sparked a sermon in you and you have no need to read any further. Wonderful! But, if you are like many preachers, you are desperate to find something new in this text that will continue to inspire you and your congregation.

I suggest choosing one small but mighty verse as the focus of your sermon: "Nothing is impossible for God" (v. 37). Two of the most prominent places in scripture where we find this declaration are in the story of Abraham and Sarah in Genesis 18, and, of course, in our text for this week when Gabriel appears to Mary. Obviously, both of them are what seem like impossible birth stories. Sarah, advanced in years, will give birth to a child named Isaac, from whom will come the nation of Israel? Hilarious! ("Isaac" means laughter). Mary, a young virgin, will birth the Son of God who will redeem the world? Insane! Both stories impossible to us, but not for God.

I am surprised how many sermons I've heard on this text in Luke that simply gloss over the empowering statement "Nothing is impossible for God." Yes, the verse is often mentioned in sermons but usually as an afterthought. "The story sounds ridiculous, but remember the angel said that nothing is impossible for God." And that's usually the end of it. Here is an idea: Why not use this verse as a refrain throughout your sermon as you share stories and testimonies that bear witness to God doing the impossible?

Approaching your sermon this way may require a change in form or structure. If you are accustomed to preaching deductive or linear sermons, perhaps it's time for something new. Why not have your sermon take the congregation for a glorious walk around this encouraging verse. Sometimes our sermons need to slow down and take time to celebrate the mighty acts of God. Affirming that "nothing is impossible for God" certainly qualifies as a celebration! Read and listen to sermons by African American preachers whose sermons often take a non-linear form, celebrating a characteristic of God.

Fred Craddock said that verse 37 is "one of those statements that's true without context."[5] Now, of course, your sermon should give the context of the verse but make it the jumping-off point to the various ways the statement continues to be true. You could begin your sermon by describing the stories of Sarah and Mary. Then let those narratives propel you into sharing stories and experiences in your life and the life of others when God pulled off the impossible. After each example is shared, repeat the verse, "Nothing is impossible for God!" If you choose to use this text on Christmas Eve, what could be more helpful or inspiring for your crowded sanctuary than examples of how God continues to work wonders in and through us?

Perhaps it is time for a bit of personal testimony. Obviously, we should be careful how often we talk about ourselves in our sermons and use discretion, but from time to time it does our congregations a world of good to hear how God helped us overcome our own challenges. We must be sensitive to those who have prayed for miracles with no success or hoped for the impossible from God and were disappointed. But aren't we supposed to let our light shine in the darkness? Just because we don't know the answers to all of the mysteries of faith does not mean we should be shy about reminding the world that we have a God who can do the impossible—Emmanuel, God with us, has come to redeem the world! Christmas reminds us that "nothing is impossible for God."

Bringing the Text to Life

My wife and I were in our early forties. We had resigned ourselves to the fact that we could not have children. All the doctors told us it was impossible. After eighteen years of marriage we were settling in to being the crazy aunt and uncle. One Sunday afternoon I came home from church and my wife said, "I'm pregnant!" "Impossible," I said. Evidently, not for God.

There was once a pastor who was appointed to a church that was known for chewing up pastors and spitting them out. His first year at the church was a difficult one. The second one was even worse because his wife was diagnosed with cancer. The wind blew in a different direction and the congregation rallied around the pastor, his wife, and family. A year later she went into remission and there was a loving bond between the pastor's family and this "difficult" congregation that lasted until he retired from that church 20 years later. He said it was the best congregation he ever served. "Nothing is impossible for God."

She didn't think she could ever give up alcohol. Truthfully, she believed it would eventually kill her. One day she accidentally bumped into a woman at a Starbucks and spilled her coffee all over the floor. Surprisingly, the whole ordeal led them to become good friends. A short time later her new friend invited her to an AA meeting. That was ten years ago. She is still sober. "Nothing is impossible for God."

December 25, 2023– Christmas Day

*Isaiah 62:6-12; Psalm 97; Titus 3:4-7; Luke 2:1-20 or **Luke 2:8-20***

Charley Reeb

Preacher to Preacher Prayer

Almighty God, on this sacred day we are in awe of your relentless love for us. Today, we celebrate that you stopped at nothing to demonstrate your love for the world. You could've chosen other means to communicate with us, but you decided to empty yourself of all your power and glory and became one of us so there would be no doubt that you are a loving, gracious, and merciful, God. Desperately we reached out for you only to find you reaching out to us in Christ. Amen.

Commentary

Every time I read our gospel text for this week I think that God could've used some help in the marketing department. Really! If God had asked you to help him spread the news that he was coming to visit the earth, what would you do? Buy television time, let the President know, post it all over social media, put it on billboards, make a movie about it, and have the angels hold a concert in big arenas across the globe and give out free tickets. God had every resource at his disposal to create the best campaign in the world. Instead, God sent his flock of angels not to religious leaders, world leaders, educators, or politicians but to the most ragtag people on earth—shepherds. I can imagine the angel Gabriel saying to God, "God, with all due respect, you want to think this through?"

Most depictions of the shepherds in the Christmas story make them look dignified. There appears to be a warm glow around them. The truth of the matter is that there was probably a stench emanating from them. At the time of Jesus's birth, shepherds were considered "low class" at best. Most folks saw them as outcasts and misfits. Bathing was not one of their priorities and they were considered untrustworthy. To the religious community, they were spiritually unclean and not allowed to participate in sacred ceremonies and holy days. And these are the ones God chose to announce the greatest event in history?

Knowing the rest of the story, we shouldn't be surprised by God's peculiar approach to announcing the birth of Christ. Jesus's ministry was defined by the attention he gave to the least, the last, and the lost—to people like the shepherds. Yes, the announcement connects Jesus to David, the shepherd who became king. But, for Luke, those invited to the Kingdom banquet are the very people who would never be invited to any party. This is why Luke has the shepherds take center stage. Just imagine the joy of the shepherds! For the first time in their lives, they mattered! For the first time in their lives, they felt important. They had moved from forgotten to unforgettable, from misfits to messengers, from overlooked to overjoyed.

The world overlooked the shepherds but God did not. The world overlooked a common manger for the King of Kings but the shepherds did not. One of the forgotten messages of Christmas is that Jesus is found in people and places the world has overlooked. Christmas is God's call to care for those who have been forgotten and ignored.

Bringing the Text to Life

There is a great deal you can do in your sermon if you choose the theme mentioned in the commentary. You can draw from a host of illustrations of admired people, both known and unknown, who have given voice to the voiceless and brought dignity and justice to those who have been cast aside. You may also engage your listeners by sharing personal stories of when you felt overlooked or ignored. All of us have been through that experience. I am sure you can also recall moments when someone took notice of you and treated you with respect and dignity. Don't forget there will be some people attending your worship service who are alone at Christmas and feel left out and overlooked. Why not share those experiences and examples in your sermon and connect them with the attention God gave to the shepherds?

I will never forget when someone important took notice of me. I had just finished playing a round of golf with my in-laws at Bay Hill Country Club in Florida, which happened to be Arnold Palmer's personal playground. At the end of our round, my in-laws stopped into the pro shop to purchase some merchandise while I sat outside waiting for them. I noticed a golf cart zip around a corner and park in front of me. When I saw who got out of the cart, my jaw dropped. It was the King of Golf himself, Arnold Palmer! He looked like he was in a hurry, so I decided not to bother him. He walked up the stairs and instead of entering the pro shop, he stopped, looked over to me, and reached out his hand to shake mine. "Hey there! Welcome to Bay Hill!" he said. "Did you enjoy the course?" I couldn't believe it. Arnold Palmer was talking to me! Honestly, I was so nervous that I can't recall what I said to him, but I will never forget that moment as long as I live. I had met the King of Golf face to face and he had taken time to have a conversation with me. He could've easily ignored me. I was just another golfer, a fan. Instead, Mr. Palmer took the time and made me feel important.

Read through the Gospels and observe how many times the King of Kings gives time and attention to those who were often ignored or cast aside. The announcement to the shepherds about the birth of Jesus was a foreshadowing of the kind of King who had come into the world.

December 31, 2023–First Sunday After Christmas Day

Isaiah 61:10-62:3; Psalm 147; Galatians 3:23-25; 4:4-7; **John 1:1-18**

Charley Reeb

Preacher to Preacher Prayer

O God, our minds can't begin to understand the height, depth, and breadth of who you are. Left to ourselves, we are lost in an eternal maze, grasping at understanding your nature and purpose for this world. Thankfully, you have made yourself known to us in the person of Jesus Christ. We are secured and comforted by your love demonstrated through the incarnation. We are forever grateful that you made your "home among us" (John 1:14).

Commentary

The prologue to John's Gospel is one of the most profound passages we find in the Bible. John doesn't bother with Mary, shepherds, wise men, or angels singing. Instead, the writer of John simply begins with Jesus (fans of Karl Barth would agree with this approach!). Matthew and Luke may tell the wondrous story of the incarnation but John takes a more theological approach. Who is Jesus exactly? Where did he come from? And why did he bother to get involved with this crazy world? John's unique perspective and language have forever dubbed it the "maverick gospel."

Clearly, the Word or *Logos* (in Greek) plays a central role in John's prologue. It is a powerful way of understanding Jesus. In addition to "word," *logos* can also mean "mind." So, one way of understanding John 1:14, "The Word became flesh" is "The mind of God became a person."[6] If you want to know the mind, heart, and personality of God, look at Jesus. In the very beginning of his Gospel, the writer of John wants to make clear that Jesus is the personification of God. God penetrated the earth in Jesus and the world has never been the same.

Many years ago, when I was a guest speaker at a college, a student boldly asked me, "Why are you a Christian? There are so many beautiful religions in the world. Why do you follow Jesus?" My answer: "I am a Christian because 'The Word became flesh and made his home among us'" (John 1:14). The student gave me a confused look. I continued, "You see, I believe God put skin on in Jesus to show you and me how much God loves us. Religion is reaching for God, but Jesus is God reaching for us. That's why I'm a Christian."[7]

The Sunday after Christmas may be a good time to remind your congregation of the theological implications of the incarnation. Throughout the season many of us have heard and sung about "Emmanuel—God with us," but perhaps we need some time to think through the real meaning and power of those words as we approach a new year. Will we face the new year with fear or uncertainty, or will we embrace the truth of Christmas and live confidently by faith knowing we can rely on God's love which desires to make its home in our hearts?

Bringing the Text to Life

Every few years religious surveys reveal that a large percentage of people believe in God or some "higher power." Many are encouraged by these surveys, but the question is "What kind of God do we believe in?" We must know the character of the God we choose to trust.

Several years ago, I recall taking our dog out before going to bed. As I was waiting for her on our screened-in porch, I heard a flutter behind me. When I turned around, there was a screech owl perched on one of our patio chairs. Its big eyes were just staring at me. It was a beautiful creature. I wondered what it was doing on my porch. Soon it dawned on me that it could not find its way out. The whole porch was surrounded by a screen, and the only way out was through a screened door that was usually left open. It was clear that it flew in through that open door but could not find the door again to get out.

The first thing I did was point to the open door, as if the owl understood human behavior. The owl kept looking at me with those big eyes. The next thing I did was walk outside the door and try to wave the owl out, "This way! This way!" The owl continued to stare at me. Then I remembered that the porch lights were not on, so I turned them on, and the owl just continued to stare at me. I finally gave up.

As I was walking up the stairs to bed, I thought, "The only way I could free that owl and bring it home is to become an owl myself."

Isn't that what God has done in Christ? God became one of us to show us the way home. "The Word became flesh" to set us free. The message of Christ is that God will stop at nothing to show us the depth of his love for us. (If you are wondering about the owl, the next morning it was gone. Perhaps another owl showed up and set it free?)

When my wife was pregnant, everyone who had kids of their own was quick to tell us that our lives were about to change. I would respond, "I know, I know." I understood it intellectually, but it wasn't until our child was born that I realized that our lives would never be the same. Our needs and desires took a back seat to the needs of our child. Since this baby was our top priority, many sacrifices were required. Our love for our child demanded it.

Jesus has been born. Has anything changed for us? Does the birth of Jesus cause us to live differently? Are we making any sacrifices? I guess it all depends on if we have made Jesus a priority. Is Christmas just a favorite holiday or is it the very reason our lives are a witness to God's love?

Listening must precede preaching. We preach because we have something to say, but we have something to say because God first speaks to us. In the following excerpt, Willimon reminds us that good sermons are the fruit of careful listening. As you read, ask yourself, "Are my sermons a reflection of the time I have spent listening for God in the text? Am I also listening to my listeners?"

—Charley Reeb, general editor

God in Conversation

Excerpt from *Listeners Dare: Hearing God in the Sermon* [1] by Will Willimon

> *The word is near you, in your mouth and in your heart (that is, the message of faith that we preach) . . . The scripture says, All who have faith in him won't be put to shame. . . . All who call on the Lord's name will be saved. So how can they call on someone they don't have faith in? And how can they have faith in someone they haven't heard of? And how can they hear without a preacher? . . . So, faith comes from listening, but it's listening by means of Christ's message. But I ask you, didn't they hear it? Definitely! Their voice has gone out into the entire earth, and their message has gone out to the corners of the inhabited world. . . . And Isaiah even dares to say, I was found by those who didn't look for me; I revealed myself to those who didn't ask for me. (Rom 10:8, 11, 13, 15, 17-20)*

Faith comes from listening (Rom 10:17). A Christian is somebody who has dared listen and then to live the Good News. The major difference between a Christian and a not-yet-Christian? The Christian has received news the non-Christian has yet to hear.

We are as we hear. "Tell me who you listen to for your daily news," said the pollster, "and I can predict your stand on a dozen issues."

Acoustically generated, Christianity is training in empty-handed receptivity. "We have heard it, God, with our own ears; our ancestors told us about it: about the deeds you did in their days, in days long past" (Ps 44:1). Nobody is born knowing either Chemistry or Christ. Want to be a chemist? Find somebody to speak the mysteries of the Periodic Table until you hear and assimilate what you've heard. Teachers of Chemistry must hand over their stuff with skill, but receivers also bear responsibility to be receptive to the truths of Chemistry, submitting to the practices of chemists, internalizing the moves. To claim with credibility, "I'm a chemist," is also to say, "I've been a good listener."

So with Christianity: Hearing of the faith precedes believing and performing the faith.

Not sure what to think about Jesus? Don't worry. He makes relationship with you his self-assignment, loves to talk, can't be shut up, even by a crucifixion, and promises in the end to have his say. The last word on your status with God is his. Your best hope is that he'll keep talking, refusing to be stumped by lousy listening.

That sermon is "good," which spurs performance as listeners become hearers who turn out to be actors. In all times and places, notwithstanding the many impediments for reception of the gospel, millions have shamelessly stepped on stage and assumed their role in Christ's drama of salvation with no justification for their risky performance than news they have heard.

Jesus took preaching as his main job, then turned around and made proclamation the vocation of all disciples (Matt 10:5-7), commanding us to tell the world news that the world can't tell itself. Sometimes with a self-effacing whisper, occasionally with a defiant, exuberant shout (Matt 10:27), all Christians must hand over what we've heard. "Tell the next generation all about the praise due the Lord and his strength—the wondrous works God has done" (Ps 78:4). "You are witnesses of these things," Christ preaching to you so that you'll be a witness who proclaims Christ to others (1 John 1:1–3), speaking out, acting up in Jesus' name when God gives you the chance.

Somebody at work says, "You're an intelligent person, so how can you fall for all that Jesus stuff?" Or, "I used to go to church every now and again, but then I realized that the church is full of homophobic, racist people, and I just don't believe in that."

You buy time saying, "I'd like to hear more," as you pray, *Lord, thanks for the thousand sermons I've sat through that prepared me for this moment.*

Don't want to be a preacher? Jesus doesn't care; all who sign on with Jesus are commissioned to speak the news they have received to others who've heard and to those who haven't. Sorry, if that wasn't made clear at your baptism.

Though we preachers love to blame our failures upon our lousy listeners, truth to tell, many listeners report frustration at their preacher's failure to help them move from listening to hearing, really hearing, and then doing the word. Listeners help God craft better preachers.

> He owned a hardware store. . . . Someone had warned me about him when I moved there. "He's usually quiet," they said, "but be careful." People still recalled the Sunday in 1970 when, in the middle of the sermon (the previous preacher's weekly diatribe against Nixon and the Vietnam War), he had stood up from where he was sitting, shook his head, and walked right out. So, I always preached with one eye on my notes and the other on him. He hadn't walked out on a sermon in more than ten years. Still, a preacher can never be too safe.
>
> You can imagine my fear when one Sunday, having waited until everyone

had shaken my hand and left the narthex, he approached me, gritting his teeth and muttering, "I just don't see things your way, preacher."

I moved into my best mode of non-defensive defensiveness, assuring him that my sermon was just one way of looking at things, and that perhaps he had misinterpreted what I said, and even if he had not, I could very well be wrong and er, uh . . .

"Don't you back off with me," he snapped. "I just said that your sermon shook me up. I didn't ask you to take it back. Stick by your guns—if you're a real preacher."

Then he said to me, with an almost desperate tone, "Preacher, I run a hardware store. Since you've never had a real job, let me explain it to you. Now, you can learn to run a hardware store in about six months. I've been there *fifteen years*. That means that all week, nobody talks to me like I know anything. I'm not like you, don't get to sit around and read books and talk about important things. It's just me and that hardware store. Sunday morning and your sermons are all I've got. Please, don't you dare take it back."[2]

Good preachers must have well-tuned ears; we're able to preach only what we have been enabled to hear. Just like you listeners, preachers are Christian on the basis of news we have heard. Discipleship is not self-sustainable; only through doggedly persistent, patient, prolonged, Sunday-after-Sunday listening do any of us stay Christian.

That's why this book is for both preachers and listeners, listeners all.

Read the rest of the book to learn more and to build your knowledge and skill as a preacher. You will find *Listeners Dare: Hearing God in the Sermon* along with many other resources for preachers and pastors at www.cokesbury.com or your favorite bookseller.

You cannot separate the sermon from the preacher. A sermon embodies the personality and leadership qualities of the preacher. Have you ever thought about how your leadership style is reflected in your preaching? The following excerpt from Lewis will help us be more intentional about integrating who we are as leaders with what and how we preach.

—Charley Reeb, general editor

Embody

Excerpt from *Embody: Five Keys to Leading with Integrity*[1] by Karoline M. Lewis

Beware of turning into the enemy you most fear. All it takes is to lash out violently at someone who has done you some grievous harm, proclaiming that only your pain matters in this world. More than against that person's body, you will then, at that moment, be committing a crime against your own imagination.

—Ariel Dorfman

In the following chapters you'll learn five keys for theological integrity in leadership. Included in each chapter is a section for further reflection that offers questions and exercises for both individual and group attention. These five keys are born out of the primary activities of the *paraclete* in John's Gospel that are then embodied in the discipleship of five women characters in John. These five bodies bear witness to God's revelation in Jesus Christ. When leaders in the church imagine themselves as paracletes, then it is these five keys that can be manifested in how they lead: accompaniment, attentiveness, authenticity, abundance, and advocacy. Each chapter begins with *observations* that present fundamental assumptions of the key being discussed, particularly against the backdrop of contemporary leadership discussions. Next, each chapter has a section devoted to *theological premises*, which situates the chapter's key principle in the wider framework of God's nature and activity, especially on the foundation of the incarnation. The third section of each chapter is a discussion of where we see that chapter's key at work specifically in the presence and portrait of the *paraclete*. The fourth section examines how a *woman character* in the Gospel of John embodies the suggested key component of leadership. Finally, each chapter concludes with *further reflection* that provides a list of exercises, questions, and readings for additional consideration about how to imagine embodying these five key aspects of the *paraclete* in our leadership.

How we engage with scripture for the sake of embodied leadership is critical. As Luke Timothy Johnson writes, "Scripture's use of body language urges us to think more constructively about what Scripture suggests about human bodies generally in connection with knowing the world and knowing God—that is, what it has to say about human bodies as medium of revelation."[2] John's Gospel takes seriously the nature of these embodied encounters between Jesus and the five women we will meet in the Fourth Gospel. Their experiences of Jesus lead to their own embodiment of who Jesus is. Johnson notes: "Scripture has been reduced to a storehouse of propositions from which deductions can be made, rather than a collection of witnesses that also enable believers to witness to God's work and glorify God's presence among them."[3] These five women in John's Gospel—the mother of Jesus, the Samaritan woman at the well, Martha, Mary, and Mary Magdalene—witness to what embodying the *paraclete* looks like. The discussions of these extraordinary women are meant to illustrate the key at work in each woman's character, thus providing a textual study for individuals or groups working through the material provided in this book.

"Authentic faith is more than a matter of right belief; it is the response of human beings in trust and obedience to the one whom Scripture designates as the Living God, in contrast to the dead idols that are constructed by humans as projections of their own desires."[4] Leadership in the church should strive for this kind of authentic faith; the church should strive for leadership that does not subscribe to human constructions of leadership and human attempts to fit a Spirit-filled church into a human-made ideal, but leadership that looks for the living God at work in the church, for the sake of the world. A focus on embodiment is not the only way to imagine leadership in the church, but it can be a significant means to stay true to the full promise of the incarnation in how we lead. Leadership in the church is distinct when it witnesses to a present God, when how we lead is not governed by a set of principles but is born out of encounters with the living God in Jesus Christ.

Embodiment also means that we make a shift from talking about leadership to talking about leaders. Leadership is an abstract concept that can easily take on characteristics all on its own without ever being connected to incarnated realities and truths. It is unhelpful to talk about leadership in the third person. Once we use the word *leader*, then we can attach it to a person. That is, "What kind of leader is she?" is a different question altogether than, "What kind of leadership traits does she have?"

Trust in the incarnation means that Jesus literally incorporated and incarnated the descriptors we use for God. The theological vocabulary we like to use when it comes to denominational identity means nothing if then not acted out, performed, and experienced. For example, consider the word *grace* and its pan-denominational use in the church. Much effort is extended toward defining *grace* without reaching any consensus. *Grace* is mercy, love, and steadfastness—to name only a few words used to define *grace*. This makes sense because we are talking about God's grace after all, and to insist on a particular or singular descriptor for *grace* would then lead to making a similar assumption about what might be possible about God.

Of course, *grace* is used extensively in the New Testament, albeit with differing definitions at work, depending on the author. The use of *grace* in the Gospel of John, however, illustrates the move from a third-person reference or definition to a first-person embodiment. In the Gospel of John, the word *grace* is used only four times and is only used in the prologue (John 1:1-18 [vv. 14, 16, and 17]). The prologue presents essential theological themes that are then unpacked in the rest of the narrative; in particular, theological themes related to Jesus's origin and Jesus's identity. This cosmic birth story, if you will, is presented in a third-person discourse, laying out certain principles that are both assumed and demonstrated or validated as the story progresses. Because of the fundamental theological premise of the incarnation, however, these theological statements cannot be left in the abstract as merely descriptive of God's revelation in Jesus. The Word becoming flesh (John 1:14) means that God assumed a new identity. God is now ontologically different and that makes a difference for how God then reveals God's very self.

As a result, what follows after the prologue is a set of claims made about God, and most directly, claims that the Word from the beginning is now flesh, is enfleshed, and embodied. From John 1:19 onward, there is a fundamental shift in how the narrative even feels. The tone is altogether different, going from explanation to incarnation.

Once the Gospel establishes that the Word has become flesh, therefore, the rest of the Gospel narrates not what grace means but how grace is experienced. The Gospel of John manifests a kind of tension between principles and praxis. *Grace* is no longer defined because it is now definitively among us, abiding with us. After John 1:17, the word *grace* never again appears in the entire Gospel of John because grace is no longer a concept but an experience. As such, having a relationship with Jesus is grace in and of itself, and as soon as we go down the road of trying to explain or define this relationship, we have missed the point altogether.

Our tendency as church leaders is to carry on as if sound theological credibility were essential to our credibility, when in fact, systematic theology is oxymoronic idolatry.[5] The systemization of theology is an act of idolatry because we have privileged the categorization of God over the knowing of God. But when the incarnation is front and center as a Christian leader, then we begin to realize that what we do and who we are must be indistinguishable.

We have a penchant to equate scripture with the living God, when scripture actually invites witness to the living God. This changes our hermeneutical approach. The five women characters we will encounter embody who Jesus is as a leader. As Johnson writes in *The Revelatory Body*, "From the beginning, Scripture functioned as a participation in the process of revelation."[6] These characters embody experiences of revelation. It is up to leaders in the church to commit to embodiment and to lead embodiedly, otherwise "theology remains a discipline concerned above all with texts and propositions based in the past, rather than discernment of the work of the Living God in the present."[7]

Your Story

Before you continue, take this moment to reflect about yourself as a leader. What characteristics immediately come to mind, and why? Are these traits you have determined for yourself, or how others have described you? Have they been ascertained by certain leadership analyses or tests? Are they characteristics outlined in a book that you were told to read? Are you able to connect these characteristics to central aspects of who you are and who you know yourself to be? Or, are these qualities more surface descriptions of what you can do, or of kinds of tasks you are able to accomplish? More importantly, can you associate these leadership skills or characteristics directly to your theological commitments? Do any of them actually originate from a belief in God you hold dear? Or do you sense a disconnect and a feeling of disembodied leadership, either because you are acting based on others' expectations or because you cannot, as hard as you try, attach these attributes to what is at stake for you theologically?

Ask yourself these questions: Why are you reading this book? What do you feel is lacking in your leadership? It is important to be able to name your motivations for wanting to dedicate your time and efforts to your identity as a leader so that you can have a sense of change or transformation after doing the work. Some additional questions that will be important to ask are: What is the core reason for picking up this book? Do you have an awareness of some discomfort or disease? Do you have the impression that your leadership is in need of either a reboot or a renewal? What and where are the points of perceived change? Or, perhaps you may be sensing that there has been an event, or a series of events or issues, that has intimated a need for a kind of reorientation in who you are as a leader. Often, such an identified event is a crisis moment, when your leadership has been questioned, or when the structures on which you have relied are no longer valid. The COVID-19 pandemic is one example of the unprecedented leadership challenges that result from crisis moments.

The following are some axles of transformation, among which you might be able to trace an advancement in how you think about your leadership and how you want to lead. If none of these axles resonate with you, document your own desires for movement:

Uncertainty—Confidence
Compartmentalization—Connection
Trapped—Liberated
Feeling silenced—Finding Your Voice
Disembodied—Embodiment
Fear—Joy
Lack of distinctiveness—Potential Realized

Tracking movement in your feelings about, and perceptions of, your leadership will result in tangible change. When change is tangible, then it can be embodied in how you go about leading. You will feel different and others will sense that difference. In other words, in order to move toward embodied change, you have to embody that transformation along the way. There needs to be actual moments and experiences in which you sense and know in your entire being that something is changed. That is what it means to be embodied and to commit to embodiment.

As noted above, the five chapters set out five keys of Christian leadership: accompaniment, attentiveness, authenticity, abundance, and advocacy. While these biblical descriptors are critical for the Christian leader, they also provide an operating hermeneutic, both to bring to scripture and to make sense of the world. That is, the Christian leader actively looks for ways in which these manifestations of God's being are present in the biblical witness and in the living witness of God's people here and now; then Christian leaders seek to embody these very principles in every aspect of leading the Christian communities to which they are called.

Read the rest of the book to learn more and to build your knowledge and skill as a preacher. You will find *Embody: Five Keys to Leading with Integrity* along with many other resources for preachers and pastors at www.cokesbury.com or your favorite bookseller.

The following excerpt from Frank Thomas shows us just how much Abraham Lincoln can teach us about being better preachers. Thomas shares a fascinating rhetorical and theological analysis of Lincoln's famous Second Inaugural. Pay special attention to how God is reflected in the address.

—Charley Reeb, general editor

The God Revealed in Lincoln's Second Inaugural Address

Excerpt from *The God of the Dangerous Sermon* [1]
by Frank A. Thomas

An American seminal figure led our nation through the Civil War of 1861–1865, the greatest threat to the American experiment the nation has ever known. More than a century and a half since his tragic death, the interest in and publication about Abraham Lincoln continues unabated. Lincoln grappled intensely with several of the most pernicious, pervasive, and persistent moral issues of the American experiment: slavery, race, and religion. The constellation of these issues expressed themselves in secession from the Union by the South, the resulting civil war, and, finally, the reconstruction of the nation after the North at long last prevailed. Based in the vast death and destruction that ensued, Lincoln sought to give the war meaning by clarifying its cause and the Christian God's role and purpose. In summary of this enormous moral struggle, religion historian Harry S. Stout labeled Lincoln "the martyred prophet . . . the theologian of reconciliation." [2] Lincoln attempted to chart an imaginative course for the nation by responding to the moral question: what does it mean to live together after violence, war, and unparalleled death with justice, reconciliation, peace, and forgiveness?

Undoubtedly, some of the fascination has been that Lincoln's life was cut short by an assassin's bullet. There was a near deification of Lincoln by many, especially in the African American community, which labeled Lincoln "Father Abraham," "the Great Emancipator," and the like. The fact that Lincoln was shot on Good Friday added to the sense that God had ordained his life and death. Our goal herein is not to deify or vilify Lincoln, but to explore his example as a flawed human being who in a time of overwhelming crisis grew and developed and was morally imaginative at a profound level. While Lincoln was a conservative thinker before the war, as James Tackach says, "a politically and intellectually cautious man by nature," he had the ability to question his "fixed attitudes on slavery, race, and religion, and other key issues of his time."[3] The result was significant personal growth and transformation, and the enlargement of his moral imagination. Many scholars have identified this capacity for self-examination and growth as one of Lincoln's most remarkable traits. David Herbert Donald suggests that Lincoln's enormous capacity for growth

> enabled one of the least experienced and most poorly prepared men ever elected to high office to become the greatest American President. Richard N. Current concurs: "[T]he most remarkable thing about him [Lincoln] was his tremendous power of growth. He grew in sympathy, in the breath of his humaneness, as he grew in other aspects of his mind and spirit." . . . Lincoln's capacity for growth and change helps reconcile those conflicting images of Lincoln—a racist to some and a champion of civil rights for others: "The one view reflects the position he started from, the other the position he was moving toward."[4]

Lincoln's massive growth and transformation in the midst of the moral dilemmas of slavery, race, and religion makes him relevant today. America is still grappling with virtually the same issues: slavery in the form of institutionalized racism, race in the form of racial equality, and religion in the form of whose religious beliefs can dominate the public square. The same need for moral imagination exists today. This motivates me to study Lincoln's life, thoughts, and for our purposes herein, theology and rhetoric. I want to look at Lincoln's moral imagination as expressed in the Second Inaugural Address and, specifically, the God of the Dangerous Sermon behind that address. Through a close reading of the address, I hope to demonstrate that out of his moral imagination Lincoln proclaimed a living, just, and universal God of healing and reconciliation rather than a tribal God of sectionalism and factionalism.

Let me respond to a question that might be lingering in the minds of many readers: how can a study of a presidential address be positioned in a homiletics textbook? Underneath this first question might be a second question: how does the study of a political speech make one a better preacher?

First, the rhetorical theology that I seek to define herein studies all "sacred rhetoric." Sacred rhetoric is any form of oratory wherein the speaker uses language and/or symbols of God in the attempt to address or persuade an audience. The orator is appealing to a God who can be characteristically discerned by a rhetorical read of the very language, symbols, metaphors, and the speaker's call to action. The speaker summons the audience to imitate and become like this God. This reflection on sacred rhetoric helps us as preachers to carefully think through and discern the language, symbols, and metaphors that we utilize when we preach and the God we are appealing to and asking the congregation to imitate in our sermons. Any oration that makes God claims or appeals to a God is worthy of study by any adherent of rhetorical theology.

Second, many scholars agree that the Second Inaugural was a sermon in all but name. At a reception at the White House following it, Lincoln asked Frederick Douglass for his opinion of the speech. Douglass replied, "Mr. Lincoln, that was a sacred effort." Later Douglass explained, "the address sounded more like a sermon than a state paper."[5] Stout remarks, "like Martin Luther King Jr.'s 'I Have a Dream' speech, the cadences, phraseology, biblical illusions, and deep moral stirrings bespeak more the pulpit than the podium."[6] Stout compares the Second Inaugural to what he regards as America's greatest sermon, Jonathan Edwards's "Sinners in the Hands of an Angry God." Several other scholars agree that, though Lincoln was not a preacher, the Second Inaugural is a sermon to the nation and the world.

Third, as Stout astutely picks up, in the study of the Second Inaugural, scholars have missed how closely Lincoln upheld the sermonic form of the Puritan jeremiad sermon. For a more detailed discussion of the Puritan, American, African American, and secular Jeremiad, please review my discussion in *American Dream 2.0.*[7]

Rhetorical Analysis of the Second Inaugural

By the time of the Second Inaugural, March 4, 1865, Lincoln was a beleaguered president. While he had been lambasted by critics in Congress and the press for much of the war, he would offer this Second Inaugural with his leadership vindicated by victory in the field. He was beginning to receive praise and credit. Because Lincoln believed the South never legally seceded from the Union, he advocated for forgiveness and "reconstruction." In 1863, Lincoln issued the Proclamation of Amnesty and Reconstruction, which openly declared his determination to reunify the North and South. Lincoln hoped that the proclamation would rally Northern support for the war and persuade weary Confederate soldiers to surrender. Lincoln's allowance of colored soldiers to fight in the Union Army and the 1863 Emancipation Proclamation brought coloreds, free and slave, to the Union cause in droves. Ultimately they were vital in helping the North to win the war. By 1865, it was clear that the United States government and the Union Army had all but prevailed. It was not personal vindication that Lincoln was after, but the Union and reunification. The moral vision of one democratic nation again consumed his heart, passion, and purpose as a leader. A president singularly and uncompromisingly committed to the purpose of preserving the Union penned the Second Inaugural address to begin to heal the wounds of the nation.

Lincoln had before him a difficult task requiring the heights and depths of the growth and transformation of his moral imagination. Losses from war were taking a huge toll on families everywhere; an estimated 623,000 people died in the Civil War. The death of so many fathers, brothers, husbands, and sons on both sides garnered incalculable grief. What did victory and defeat mean in the shadow of so costly and great a tragedy? Would the president advocate for immediate implementation of Reconstruction? What about the four million slaves who were now "free"? What would be done concerning the matter of their suffrage? Would they now be full American citizens? Would Lincoln offer a triumphant victory speech castigating the South for its recalcitrance and the sin of slavery? Would he really follow through on reconstruction and forgiveness, or were the Confederates to be treated as a conquered nation? Would the Confederacy's civic and military leaders be charged with treason? Or was there some other vision or course the president would set for the nation? Without question, there was wide interest, speculation, and concern as to exactly what Abraham Lincoln would say.

I have divided the speech into three movements, the first "No prediction is ventured," the second "All dreaded it—all sought to avert it," and the final "malice toward none; with charity for all."

Movement One: "No prediction is ventured"

Lincoln begins the speech in subdued and somber tones with the term "Fellow Countrymen." His purpose is to discuss the deeper moral cause and meaning of the war, but to move to such depth of thought, he has to re-set audience expectation. He is clear in this first movement as to what the speech is not, in order to set up the deeper conversation. He changes audience expectation by using the qualifying language of *less*, *little*, and *no*. He says, at this "second appearing" [Second Inaugural] there is "*less* occasion for an extended address than there was at the first [Inaugural]."[8] So much had been said that "*little* that is new that could be presented about the great contest." The nation had talked about the war ad infinitum in the last four years and he could not add anything new to the discussion. Therefore, in contradistinction to vast audience expectation, the speech would offer *no* information on the war per se. Also, given the fact that victory for the North seemed imminent, there would be no discussion of restoring the nation on the Union's exclusive terms: no revelry, triumphalism, or celebration of victory, and especially no discussion of treason and punishment for the South. Lincoln offered no specific policy proposals and platitudes about the greatness of America and its government. This was to be a very different inaugural than the traditional and standard inaugural speech.

Again, Lincoln wants to discuss national issues of great moral struggle, such as what did God demand of the nation that Lincoln called "the last best hope of humankind"? How does the nation make sense of the slaughter and suffering other than simplistic civic and religious explanations of scapegoating the other side? How does the nation give these great sacrifices of loss and death meaning? These are moral issues that require use of imagination, the moral imagination. Lincoln's Second Inaugural is an attempt to shape the moral imagination and behavior of the nation by articulation of a theology of reconciliation based in his understanding of a universal God, the Supreme Ruler of the nations, who paid close attention to the American experiment and punished America severely for its offence of slavery. But, in the raw optimism of the American jeremiad, judgment and punishment was not the final word. Lincoln offered the nation a new and healing future for all parties involved regardless of the past.

The conversation that Lincoln was seeking to have with the nation and the world was the conversation that he had been having deep inside his own soul, expressed to this point only in private, and in the Second Inaugural for the first time in a public address. The war had gone on far longer and at a cost far higher than either side could have planned for or predicted. He ends the first paragraph and movement of the address with the statement that "with high hopes for the future," in regards to the war, "*no* prediction in regard to it is ventured."

Movement Two: "All dreaded it; all sought to avert it"

The second movement of the speech begins with a reference to the First Inaugural when Lincoln says, "all thoughts were anxiously directed to an impending civil war." Notice this is his first utilization of the term "civil war" as opposed to "great contest" in the first paragraph. He clearly begins to outline his strategy for holding the nation together. He cannot paper over the reality that the nation is at war with itself. He says, "All dreaded it—all sought to avert it." He uses *all,* and its surrogates, *both, each, neither, American,* and *toward none* to convey that the nation is one with a painful and tragic difference of opinion. Despite the violence and the bloodshed of war, the nation is not two separate peoples, necessitating language of us vs. them or North vs. South. Speaking of the civil war, he says, "*All* dreaded it—*all* sought to avert it." Lincoln's use of the word *all* and its surrogates in his language structure is symbolic of his great struggle to hold North and South together in legal, material, and spiritual reality. His language attempts to hold the nation together even as his actions do the same. Though he recognizes the division, he is not using the language of division.

His phraseology of *all* has the connotation of not only holding both sides together, but also holding them together in tension. He says that while the First Inaugural address was being devoted to saving the union without war, "insurgents" were in the city at that very time seeking to destroy the Union without war. He labels them "insurgents" who were seeking to dissolve the Union and divide the "effects" of the nation through a process of negotiation. The "all" of which Lincoln speaks is fraught with the tensions of division and difference visible in the tangible behavior of both sides in regards to the war. He continues to hold North and South in tension by stating that while *both* (a derivative of all) parties deprecated war, one of them [the South] would make war rather than let the nation survive, and the other [the North] would accept war rather than let it perish. Lincoln is clear that the *all* of which he speaks is not an idyllic *all* of harmony and good feelings, but the togetherness of a family with tension, strife, and violence.

After holding *both* sides in tension, Lincoln makes a potent statement, and a shift in preoccupation away from human actions, perspectives, and behaviors indicated by this phrase, "And the war came." He does not say the South or the North brought the war. He does not blame either side, but is careful to say, "the war came." Lincoln is suggesting that, for all the aggressive language and argument, neither side was fully in control. Ronald C. White, Jr. in his book *Lincoln's Greatest Speech: The Second Inaugural,* suggests that Lincoln looked back from the perspective of four long years and saw that, all along, the war had a life of its own. White quotes Charles Royster, who says with the scale of destruction to which the participants committed themselves to in the Civil War, "Americans surprised themselves with the extent of violence they could attain."[9] Lincoln concluded that though there were battle plans and projections, arguments and actions, in the moral and spiritual arena participants had battled in total confusion. For Lincoln, reason alone could not explain the bloodshed and violence because the level of death and destruction had grown incomprehensible. Independent of presidents, generals, soldiers, and populations, the war had a life of its own. White says that at this point in the speech, "War becomes the subject and is no longer a direct object of the action of others."[10] Lincoln now moves to discuss the direct cause of the war.

Although in the First Inaugural the purpose of the impending war was to preserve the Union, nevertheless, after four long years of war, it is clear to Lincoln that the cause of the war has shifted. Lincoln introduces slaves into the address as one-eighth of the population, mostly situated in the South. He defines them as a "peculiar and powerful [economic] interest." He returns to the subject of *all*: "*All* knew that this interest was *somehow* the cause of the war." The word *somehow* is very significant in that it suggests a sense of mystery on both sides as to how slavery became the cause of the war. Lincoln will later unfold the source of *somehow* as the hand and providence of God.

Lincoln states that the objective of the insurgents was to strengthen, perpetuate, and extend this economic interest by rending the Union even by war, while the government only wanted to restrict territorial enlargement of slavery. Notice the tension of the language of insurgents and the government. Lincoln then reverts back to holding everyone together in tension:

> *Neither* party expected for the war the magnitude or the duration. . . . *Neither* anticipated that the cause of the conflict might cease with or even before the conflict itself should cease. *Each* looked for an easier triumph and a result less fundamental and astounding. *Both* read the same Bible and pray to the same God and each invokes His aid against the other.

Neither party could anticipate the magnitude of duration of the war, nor that the initial cause for the war would be transformed. In human terms, as White says, "Lincoln was driven to the alternative of either surrendering the Union, and with it the Constitution, or of arming Southern slaves."[11] According to Lincoln's plan, the Union would be preserved first, and then the slaves would be freed. *Somehow*, a hint at divine initiative, the second step had become the first step. He returns to the sense of *all*. *Each side* in their human interest had looked for an easier triumph. *Both sides* read the same Bible, prayed to the same God, and invoked God's aid against the other. While *both sides* were certain of their own righteousness, Lincoln is setting up the reality of divine punishment and purposes rather than human plans and outcomes.

Lincoln then makes a major shift and unfolds in theological detail the true cause of the war. Lincoln quotes Genesis 3:19, where Adam and Eve had sinned, and, because of their sin, God tells Adam, "in the sweat of thy face shalt thou eat." Lincoln asks the question: How is it that anyone could ask a just God to assist in "wringing their bread from the sweat of other men's faces?" He is challenging slavery as against the biblical mandate of Genesis 3:19 (KJV). He lets the judgment linger momentarily on the South, whom most of the audience would think that he is exclusively referring to. He then quickly flips audience expectation and quotes Matthew 7:1, where Jesus in the Sermon on the Mount says, "Let us not judge, lest we be judged" (KJV). Many in the North wanted to judge, and had already judged, but he is telling them to be careful because in fact they will be under the same judgment. He is guarding against self-righteousness by those of the North, because the truth is the North had complicity in slavery. Lincoln is not interested in a tribal God who is on the side of the North or the South and who would punish one side over the other.

Because God is not a tribal God, the prayers of *both sides* against the other could not be answered and *neither side's* prayer had been fully answered because "the Almighty has his own purposes." God's purposes are something different than that of either party. Lincoln then slips back to judgment, "Woe unto the world because of offences! for it must needs be that offences come; but woe to that man by whom the offence cometh!" He is quoting Jesus in Matthew 18:3-7 (KJV):

> Except ye be converted, and become as little children, ye shall not enter into the kingdom of heaven. . . . But whoso shall offend one of these little ones which believe in me, it were better for him that a millstone were hanged about his neck. . . . Woe unto the world because of offences! for it must needs be that offence come, but woe to the man by whom the offence cometh.

Lincoln is making plain that slavery is the offence and the little ones being offended are slave populations. Slavery is one of the offences, which in God's providence must come, and will continue until God's appointed time. Lincoln surmises that God wills to remove *American* slavery (another term of *all*), and, as a result, has given the North and the South "this terrible war" as a woe for the offence. Notice, as a sign of *all*, Lincoln calls it *American* slavery and not Southern slavery. Lincoln then suggests that slavery does not line up with any attributes "which the believers in a Living God always ascribe to Him." In other words, slavery cannot be consistent with any attribute of a Living God. Lincoln offers hope and prayer:

> Fondly do we hope—fervently do we pray—that this mighty scourge of war may speedily pass away. Yet, if God wills that it continue until all the wealth piled . . . by two hundred and fifty years of unrequited toil shall be sunk and until every drop of blood drawn with the lash shall be paid by the sword, as was said three thousand years ago, so still it must be said, "the judgments of the Lord, are true and righteous altogether."

Notice the use of the word *scourge*, chastisement or punishment, most notably used in Hebrews 12:6: "for whom the Lord loves he chastens, and scourges every son whom He receives" (NKJV). Slavery has been harsh and the nation's sin has been severe, so severe that, as Tackach paraphrases Lincoln's meaning: "the war's losses were the wages of national sin, payable in both life and treasure."[12] Lincoln fully assents and submits to God's judgment, quoting Psalm 19:7–9 (KJV), "The judgments of the Lord are true and righteous altogether." In this second movement, the theme is *all*: *both* the North and South were being judged for the offence of slavery. Though *each side*, in serving their tribal God, blames, finds fault, and prays against the other, God is not on either side. God is not a tribal God.

Even in the pronouncement, of judgment, consistent with the tone and tenor of the American jeremiad, Lincoln is after reconciliation. It would not serve the cause of reconciliation if the South were burdened with the singular guilt of the war. The North was complicit as well. Tackach explains the complicity in great detail as the South cultivating slavery and the North tolerating it for its own advantage:

Thomas Jefferson's original draft of the Declaration of Independence charged King George III for waging, "a cruel war against human nature itself, violating its most sacred right of life and Liberty in the persons of a distant people who never offended him, captivating them into slavery in another hemisphere, or to incur miserable death in their transportation thither." When the representatives from the Southern slaveholding colonies protested this passage, these words were struck from the Declaration. For the sake of unity against Great Britain, the Northern colonies acquiesced to the South's peculiar institution. Again for the sake of unity, the delegates at the Philadelphia convention of 1787 chose not to create a Constitution that outlawed slavery. The Northern textile mills spun Southern cotton picked by slaves. White laborers in the border states like Indiana and Lincoln's Illinois relied on slavery to keep the Blacks out, assuring the jobs would be available for white workers and that pay scales would not fall. To preserve the union, antislavery Northerners like Daniel Webster compromised with the slave power, passing the Fugitive Slave Law and other legislation that protected slavery.[13]

The South had been articulating Northern complicity for generations. While many did not, Lincoln had the moral capacity to see that *both* North and South participated in slavery. Because of this moral capacity, Lincoln never spoke about God in the language of triumphalism. He was very suspicious of church leaders who knew exactly when, where, and how God was on their side. The bottom line was that Lincoln did not see himself as exclusively a Northern president; he was the president of the North and South.

For my purposes, the God of the Dangerous Sermon is the God revealed in Lincoln's Second Inaugural. These are the attributes of God that can be discerned from the address.

- a Living God, not a tribal or territorial God, choosing one party in the conflict over the other;
- an inclusive God, a universal God offering both judgment and reconciliation;
- a God of covenant evidenced in a relationship with America similar to that with the Hebrew nation of the Old Testament;
- a God of mercy revealed and evidenced in Jesus and his Sermon on the Mount;
- a God of evenhanded justice of the entire human race, especially those with favored status;
- a providential God whose purposes are not fully known and who is active in orchestrating human affairs towards mysterious ends;
- a God not as concerned for individual salvation per se, but for the nation as a collective;

- a God not as concerned with the theological doctrine of damnation in the afterlife, but with hell on earth;
- a God concerned for the "little ones" and the offences they receive.

Lincoln wrote to Eliza Gurney in 1862:

> We must believe that He permits it [the war] for some wise purpose of his own, mysterious and unknown to us; and though with our limited understandings we may not be able to comprehend it, yet we cannot but believe that he who made the world still governs it.[14]

Lincoln fully reveals the God of the universe, the Supreme Ruler of all nations, who holds nations and people accountable but also offers mercy, love, and reconciliation if the nations and people would accept it and act in peace and reconciliation with each other. Lincoln then explains the ethics of the Living God.

Movement Three: "With malice toward none; with charity for all"

The distinguishing factor of the American jeremiad is its optimism and hope. God in mercy in the midst of judgment ultimately offers redemption to America. Lincoln, out of his moral imagination, based in the mercy and grace of the Living God, paints a post–Civil War vision of America:

> With malice *toward none*; with charity for *all*; with firmness in the right, as God gives us to see the right, let us strive on to finish the work we are in: to bind up the nation's wounds; to care for him who shall have borne the battle, and for his widow and his orphan—to do all which may achieve and cherish a just and a lasting peace among ourselves, and with all the nations.

Lincoln holds the nation together, resolves the tension of difference, and charts a future of forgiveness and reconciliation for *all*. To overcome the desire to punish and garner revenge on the South and to deal with the South's anger and humiliation at being defeated, he suggests malice toward none. Malice is not simply evil, it is directed evil with the intent to harm and hurt. Lincoln believes malice is the ethic of a tribal God. The universal and inclusive God offers charity for *all*. Lincoln is not simply talking about unselfish love among like neighbors of the same tribe, family, party, or clan, but Jesus's radical ethic of agape love for enemies. This vision is based in a God of reconciliation and forgiveness who had been the principal actor in the Civil War. Lincoln is calling the nation to overcome the boundaries of race, regionalism, political parties, and sectarian policies to come together in reconciliation and forgiveness. Despite judgment, Lincoln believed that the Living God, who has divine, not human purposes, would renew and restore the nation back to the covenant.

Lincoln says "with firmness in the right, as God gives us to see the right." He is emphasizing the severe limitation of human righteousness. He was weary and wary of leaders, and especially church leaders, who knew that God was on their side. He had seen firsthand the harm caused by those who were absolutely sure that their purposes were right and they were acting for God. Lincoln struggled with the lack of humility in the moral lives of so many of the principal actors in the civil conflict—the hypocrisy and moral pretentiousness of those who wanted to punish the South as if the North was not complicit, and the self-righteous ministers and churches on both sides with biblical justifications of unimaginable suffering—and yet no sense that they were contributing to and making the violence possible.

Basic in the ethic of the Living God, Lincoln makes very specific appeals to finish the nation's work: "to bind up the nation's wounds; to care for him who shall have borne the battle, and for his widow and his orphan." Starting with soldiers who bore the battle and their families, so many of whom had become widows and orphans, Lincoln called forth compassion and mercy as the true test of whether the nation understood the purposes of God in the war. It was not just victory, but how one treated those who were defeated that God was careful to observe. If hostilities continued after the war and neither side learned anything, then the war would have been for naught.

Lincoln concludes with: "to do *all* which may achieve and cherish a just and lasting peace among ourselves and with *all* nations." Stout says that Lincoln believed passionately in the U.S. republic. It was his "political religion," one he hoped would be preached to the world:

> But it was not nationalism for the sake of nationalism. . . . Lincoln's was a prudential and moral nationalism. Put simply, he would have never said, "my country right or wrong." The United States, Lincoln believed, deserved reverential awe only to the extent it conformed to the higher ethical imperative contained in the principle that "all men are created equal." That is why he said repeatedly that the nation could not survive only "half slave and half free," including the territories and States in waiting, that it was a Republic not worth preserving.[15]

In summary, Lincoln believed the nation had sinned in the development, perpetuation, and tolerance of slavery. *All* had offended God, and God gave the "scourge" of war as corrective punishment. God offered redemption and a new path for the nation—malice toward none, binding up the nation's wounds, to care for those who have borne the battle and their widows and orphans, and to do everything to achieve a just and lasting peace, among Americans and with all nations.

Read the rest of the book to learn more and to build your knowledge and skill as a preacher. You will find *The God of the Dangerous Sermon* along with many other resources for preachers and pastors at www.cokesbury.com or your favorite bookseller

Notes

January 2023

1. Fred B. Craddock, *The Collected Sermons of Fred B. Craddock* (Louisville: Westminster John Knox Press, 2011), 96.

2. Willie James Jennings, *A Theological Commentary on the Bible: Acts* (Louisville: Westminster John Knox Press, 2017), 111–12.

3. Walter Brueggemann, *Texts for Preaching: A Lectionary Commentary, Based on the NRSV*, Vol. 1: Year A, ed. Brueggemann, Charles B. Cousar, Beverly R. Gaventa, and James D. Newsome (Louisville: Westminster John Knox Press, 1995), 101.

4. Paul Hanson, *Isaiah 40–66*, Interpretation (Louisville: John Knox Press, 2012), 128.

February 2023

1. Martin Luther King Jr., "I've Been to the Mountaintop," April 3, 1968, Memphis, Tennessee.

March 2023

1. Philip Keller, *A Shepherd Looks at Psalm 23* (Grand Rapids: Zondervan, 2015), 123.

2. Nancy R. Bowen, *Ezekiel*, Abingdon Old Testament Commentaries (Nashville: Abingdon Press), Kindle edition, 222.

3. Bowen, *Ezekiel*, 223.

4. Angela Duckworth, *Grit: The Power of Passion and Perseverance* (New York: Scribner's, 2016), 274

April 2023

1. Stanley Saunders, "Triumphal Entry," *Working Preacher*, March 29, 2015, http://www.workingpreacher.org/preaching.aspx?commentary_id=2404.

2. Rakesh Kochhar and Anthony Cilluffo, "Income Inequality in the U.S. Is Rising Most Rapidly Among Asians," *Pew Research Center*, July 12, 2018,

https://www.pewresearch.org/social-trends/2018/07/12/income-inequality-in
-the-u-s-is-rising-most-rapidly-among-asians/.

3. "The Model Minority Myth," *The Practice, Asian Americans in the Law.* Volume 5, issue 1 (November/December 2018), https://thepractice.law.harvard .edu/article/the-model-minority-myth/.

4. Isaac Watts, "When I Survey the Wondrous Cross," *United Methodist Hymnal* (Nashville: United Methodist Publishing House, 1989), 298.

5. William Barclay, *The Gospel of John*, volume 2, The Daily Study Bible Series, rev. ed. (Philadelphia: The Westminster Press, 2010), 58.

May 2023

1. *Star Trek: The Next Generation*, "Darmok," season 5, ep. 2 (1991).

June 2023

1. William Placher, *Narratives of a Vulnerable God* (Louisville: Westminster John Knox Press, 1994), 67–68.

2. Colin Gunton, *The Promise of Trinitarian Theology*, 2nd ed. (Edinburgh: T&T Clark, 1997), 2–3.

3. Placher, *Narratives of a Vulnerable God*, 71.

4. Brian W. Stolarz, *Grace and Justice on Death Row: The Race against Time and Texas to Free an Innocent Man* (New York: Skyhorse, 2016). See also Mike Tolson, "Death Row Inmate Free 12 Years Later," *Houston Chronicle*, June 13, 2015, https://www.chron.com/news/houston-texas/houston/article/Death-row -inmate-free-12-years-later-6325948.php.

July 2023

1. Stanley Cavell, *Must We Mean What We Say?: A Book of Essays* (Cambridge: Cambridge University Press, 2015), 70.

2. Herbert McCabe, *Law, Love, Language* (New York: Continuum International Publishing, 2012), 114–19.

3. Craig Hill, *In God's Time: The Bible and the Future* (Grand Rapids: Eerdmans, 2002), 4.

August 2023

1. Matthew Henry, "Genesis 37," *Complete Commentary on the Bible*, https:// www.studylight.org/commentaries/eng/mhm/-37.html.

2. "A Brief Great Thanksgiving for General Use," *United Methodist Hymnal* (Nashville: The United Methodist Publishing House, 1989), 6–11.

3. Darryl Bell, *Leadership*, vol. 5, no. 4, quoted in Mark Beaird 1-07, "God Is Leading: Are You Following?" http://markbeaird.org/wmlib/pdf/sermons/mark _beaird/god_is_leading.pdf.

September 2023

1. Henri Nouwen, *In the Name of Jesus* (Chestnut Ridge, NY: Crossroad Publishing, 1989).

2. Percy Dearmer, "Draw Us in the Spirit's Tether," *United Methodist Hymnal* (Nashville: United Methodist Hymnal, 1989), 632.

3. Dennis K. Olson, "Eighteenth Sunday after Pentecost," September 14, 2008, *Working Preacher*, http://www.workingpreacher.org/preaching .aspx?commentary_id=139

4. Benyamin Cohen, "I'd Like to Teach the World to Sing," *Torah from Dixie*, http://www.tfdixie.com/parshat/beshalach/008.htm.

5. Amy-Jill Levine, *Short Stories by Jesus: The Enigmatic Parables of a Controversial Rabbi* (New York: HarperOne, reprint ed., 2015), 76.

6. Stanley Saunders, "Commentary on Matthew 20:1-16," September 20, 2020, *Working Preacher*, https://www.workingpreacher.org/preaching .aspx?commentary_id=4574.

October 2023

1. Jeff A. Benner, *Ancient Hebrew Lexicon of the Bible* (n.p.: Virtualbookwork.com Publishing, 2005), 278.

2. Terence Fretheim, "Exodus 32:1-6, The Golden Calf," *Interpretation: Exodus*, Digital Edition, part 8, The Fall and Restoration (Louisville: Westminster John Knox Press, 2010).

3. Benner, *Ancient Hebrew Lexicon of the Bible*.

November 2023

1. Tim Urban, "Inside the Mind of a Master Procrastinator," filmed February 2016 in Vancouver, BC, TED video, 15:55, https://www.ted.com/talks /tim_urban_inside_the_mind_of_a_master_procrastinator. The picture shown in his talk is also available on his blog post, "Your Life in Weeks," May 7, 2014, https://waitbutwhy.com/2014/05/life-weeks.html.

Notes to Pages 132–157

2. *Big Fish*, directed by Tim Burton (Columbia Pictures, 2003). The swamp witch scene is about nine minutes into the movie.

December 2023

1. Christopher David, "Commentary on Isaiah 64:1-9," *Working Preacher*, November 29, 2020, https://www.workingpreacher.org/commentaries/revised -common-lectionary/first-sunday-of-advent-2/commentary-on-isaiah-641 -9-5?fbclid=IwAR23lpOSK1LPXX9UJEwcquKw6x_MlxWkfaP-grjYP5MgcL -N4z--MRQ66Zc.

2. Todd Spangler, "'The Office' Was by Far the Most-Streamed TV Show in 2020, Nielsen Says," *Variety*, January 12, 2021, https://variety.com/2021/digital /news/the-office-most-streamed-tv-show-2020-nielsen-1234883822/.

3. *Elf*, directed by John Favreau (New Line Cinema, 2003).

4. Xin Xin, "Update: You Can't Wait Until Life Isn't Hard Anymore before You Decide to Be Happy—Nightbirde." Medium.com., June 10, 2021, https:// medium.com/body-mind-soul/nightbirde-its-okay-e651ce5530f8.

5. Fred B. Craddock, *As One Without Authority* (St. Louis, Missouri: Chalice Press, 2001), 145.

6. William Barclay, *Who Is Jesus?* (Lake Junaluska, NC: The World Methodist Council, 1975), 22.

7. Charley Reeb, *Lose the Cape* (Lima, OH: CSS Publishing Company, 2019), 39, 44.

Essay: "God in Conversation"—Will Willimon

1. Will Willimon, Listeners Dare: Hearing God in the Sermon (Nashville: Abingdon Press, 2022).

2. Will Willimon, *Stories* (Nashville: Abingdon, 2020), 7–8.

Essay: "Embody"—Karoline M. Lewis

1. Karoline M. Lewis, *Embody: Five Keys to Leading with Integrity* (Nashville: Abingdon Press, 2020).

2. Luke Timothy Johnson, *The Revelatory Body: Theology as Inductive Art* (Grand Rapids: Eerdmans, 2015), 53.

3. Johnson, *The Revelatory Body*, 38.

4. Johnson, *The Revelatory Body*, 1.

5. Johnson, *The Revelatory Body*, 12.

6. Johnson, *The Revelatory Body*, 3.

7. Johnson, *The Revelatory Body*, 15.

Essay: "The God Revealed in Lincoln's Second Inaugural Address"—Frank A. Thomas

1. Frank A. Thomas, *The God of the Dangerous Sermon* (Nashville: Abingdon Press, 2021).

2. Harry S. Stout, "Abraham Lincoln as Moral Leader: The Second Inaugural as America's Sermon to the World," from *Lincoln and Leadership: Military, Political, and Religious Decision Making*, ed. Randall M. Miller (New York: Fordham University Press, 2012), 79.

3. James Tackach, *Lincoln's Moral Vision: The Second Inaugural Address* (Jackson: University of Mississippi Press, 2002), xxii.

4. Tackach, *Lincoln's Moral Vision*, xiii.

5. Stout, "Abraham Lincoln as Moral Leader," 78.

6. Stout, "Abraham Lincoln as Moral Leader," 78–79.

7. Frank A. Thomas, "The American Jeremiad and the Cultural Myth of America" in *American Dream 2.0: A Christian Way Out of the Great Recession* (Nashville: Abingdon Press, 2012), 3–15.

8. All quoted references are from "Lincoln's Second Inaugural," U.S. Department of the Interior, https://www.nps.gov/linc/learn/historyculture/lincoln-second-inaugural.htm.

9. Ronald C. White, Jr., *Lincoln's Greatest Speech: The Second Inaugural* (New York: Simon and Schuster, 2002), 78.

10. White, *Lincoln's Greatest Speech*, 12.

11. White, *Lincoln's Greatest Speech*, 82.

12. Tackach, *Lincoln's Moral Vision*, 138.

13. Tackach, *Lincoln's Moral Vision*, 136.

14. White, *Lincoln's Greatest Speech*, 142.

15. Stout, "Abraham Lincoln as Moral Leader," 92.

Contributors

Sermon Helps

Jennifer Forrester—Associate Pastor, First United Methodist Church, Hickory, North Carolina
January 1; January 8; January 15

Bill Burch—Senior Pastor, Northside United Methodist Church, Atlanta, Georgia
January 22; January 29; February 5

Robin Wilson—Interim Lead Pastor, First United Methodist Church, Dothan, Alabama
February 12; February 19; February 22

Susan Gray—Pastor, First United Methodist Church Jupiter Tequesta, Jupiter, Florida
February 26; March 5; March 12

DJ del Rosario—Pastor, Federal Way United Methodist Church, Auburn, Washington
March 19; March 25/26; April 2

Riley Short—United Methodist Minister, retired
April 6; April 7; April 9

Lynn Bartlow—Lead Pastor, St. Marks United Methodist Church, Tucson, Arizona
April 16; April 23; April 30

Ron Bartlow—Senior Pastor, St. Paul's United Methodist Church, Tucson, Arizona
May 7; May 14; May 21

Steve Price—Co-Pastor, Trinity United Methodist Church, Gainesville, Florida
May 28; June 4; June 11

Jason Micheli—Senior Pastor, Annandale United Methodist Church, Annandale, Virginia
June 18; June 25; July 2

Kevin Murriel—Senior Pastor, Cascade United Methodist Church, Atlanta, Georgia
July 9; July 16; July 23

Jeremy Squires—Pastor, Nolensville First United Methodist Church, Nashville, Tennessee
July 30; August 6; August 13

Emily Hotho—District Superintendent of the Gulf Central District of the Florida Conference UMC
August 20; August 27; September 3

Mandy Sloan McDow—Senior Minister, Los Angeles First United Methodist Church, Los Angeles, California
September 10; September 17; September 24

Roland Millington—Pastor, Brimfield United Methodist Church, Brimfield, Illinois
October 1; October 8; October 15

Dottie Escobedo-Frank—Senior Pastor, Paradise Valley United Methodist Church, Nogales, Arizona
October 22; October 29; November 1

Cyndi McDonald—Pastor, Barnesville First United Methodist Church, Barnesville, Georgia
November 5; November 12; November 19

Paul Cho—Senior Pastor, Tempe First United Methodist Church, Tempe, Arizona
November 23; November 26

David K. Johnson—Pastor, First United Methodist Church of Round Rock, Texas
December 3; December 10; December 17

Charley Reeb—Senior Pastor, Johns Creek United Methodist Church, Johns Creek, Georgia
December 24; December 25; December 31

Essays for Skill-Building

Will Willimon, the author of more than seventy-five books, is a preacher and teacher of preachers. He is a United Methodist bishop (retired) and serves as professor of the practice of Christian ministry and director of the Doctor of Ministry program at Duke Divinity School, Durham, North Carolina.

Karoline M. Lewis holds the Marbury Anderson Chair in Biblical Preaching at Luther Seminary in St. Paul, Minnesota. She is a regularly featured presenter and preacher at the Festival of Homiletics and a frequent contributor for numerous journals and resources, including the popular website WorkingPreacher.org where she co-hosts the site's weekly podcast, "Sermon Brainwave," and authors the site's weekly column, "Dear Working Preacher." She is the author of *SHE: Five Keys to Unlock the Power of Women in Ministry* and *Embody: Five Keys to Leading with Integrity*.

Thomas A. Frank is the Nettie Sweeney and Hugh Th. Miller Professor of Homiletics and Director of the Academy of Preaching and Celebration at Christian Theological Seminary in Indianapolis, Indiana. He is the author of many books, including *Introduction to the Practice of African American Preaching*.

Thematic Index

Scripture Index

Old Testament

Ecclesiastes

Song of Solomon

Isaiah

Jeremiah

Ezekiel

Joel

New Testament

Online Edition

The Abingdon Preaching Annual 2023 online edition is available by subscription at www.ministrymatters.com.

Abingdon Press is pleased to make available an online edition of *The Abingdon Preaching Annual 2023* as part of our Ministry Matters online community and resources.

Subscribers to our online edition will also have access to preaching content from prior years.

Visit www.ministrymatters.com and click on SUBSCRIBE NOW. From that menu, select "Abingdon Preaching Annual" and follow the prompt to set up an account.

If you have logged into an existing Ministry Matters account, you can subscribe to any of our online resources by simply clicking on MORE SUBSCRIPTIONS and following the prompts.

Please note, your subscription to *The Abingdon Preaching Annual* will be renewed automatically, unless you contact MinistryMatters.com to request a change.

Made in the USA
Coppell, TX
27 January 2023

11746328R00108